THE GERMAN REFORMATION

Studies in European History

Series Editors: Richard Overy
John Breuilly
Peter Wilson

Published Titles

THE GERMAN REFORMATION

Second Edition

R. W. SCRIBNER
and
C. SCOTT DIXON

First edition published 1986
Second edition published 2003 by
PALGRAVE MACMILLAN
Houndmills, Basingstoke, Hampshire RG21 6XS and
175 Fifth Avenue, New York, N.Y. 10010
Companies and representatives throughout the world

PALGRAVE MACMILLAN is the global academic imprint of the
Palgrave Macmillan division of St. Martin's Press, LLC and of
Palgrave Macmillan Ltd. Macmillan® is a registered trademark
in the United States, United Kingdom and other countries. Palgrave
is a registered trademark in the European Union and other
countries.

ISBN 0–333–66528–7 paperback

This book is printed on paper suitable for recycling and made
from fully managed and sustained forest sources.

A catalogue record for this book is available from the British Library.

Library of Congress Cataloging-in-Publication Data
Scribner, Robert W.
    The German Reformation / R.W. Scribner and
  C. Scott Dixon. – 2nd ed.
      p. cm. – (Studies in European history)
    Includes bibliographical references (p.   ) and index.
    ISBN 0–333–66528–7 (pbk.)
      1. Reformation – Germany. 2. Germany – Church history –
16th century. I. Dixon, C. Scott. II. Title. III. Studies in European history
(Basingstoke, England)

BR305.3.S37 2003
274.3′06–dc21   2003051168

10   9   8   7   6   5   4   3   2   1
12 11 10 09 08 07 06 05 04 03

Printed in China

Contents

Editor's Preface

The main purpose of this new series of studies is to make available to teacher and student alike developments in a field of history that has become increasingly specialised with the sheer volume of new research and literature now produced. These studies are designed to present the 'state of the debate' on important themes and episodes in European history since the sixteenth century, in a clear and critical way by someone who is himself closely concerned with the debate in question.

The studies are not intended to be read as extended bibliographical essays, though each will contain a detailed guide to further reading which will lead students and the general reader quickly to key publications. Each book carries its own interpretation and conclusions, while locating the discussion firmly in the centre of the current issues as historians see them. It is intended that the series will introduce students to historical approaches which are in some cases very new and which, in the normal course of things, would take many years to filter down into the textbooks and school histories. I hope it will demonstrate some of the excitement that historians, like scientists, feel as they work away in the vanguard of their subject. The series has an important contribution to make in publicising what it is that historians are doing and in making history more open and accessible. It is vital for history to communicate if it is to survive.

R. J. OVERY

Introduction

The aim of this pamphlet is to provide for student use a survey of recent work on the German Reformation. The past decade of research has seen a retreat from a narrowly confessional 'religious history' of the Reformation, and much greater discussion about the broader context of religious reform. Many new questions have been asked, about the relationship of religion to society, about the antecedents of the sixteenth-century religious reform, about how it spread and how it was received, as well as about its social and political impact. Much of this recent discussion has been concerned with the broadly 'sociological' conditions of the Reformation, although increasingly a number of anthropological questions have been explored, many under the heading of 'popular belief' or 'popular culture' (see Bibliography nos. 2–3, 9–10, 18–19). The implications of such discussion for a general interpretation of the German Reformation have not yet been drawn out, and they often find little mention in general textbooks. However, they signal a radical change in our understanding of the Reformation and its importance for early modern European history.

It is not my intention therefore to retell, yet again, the familiar story of 'Luther's break with Rome' – to retrace the question of indulgences, Tetzel, the campaign against the Papacy, Luther's condemnation at Worms, etc., etc. This is more than adequately done by traditional textbooks. Moreover, since A. G. Dickens' groundbreaking *The German Nation and Martin Luther*, it is unnecessary to apologise for addressing issues in a general text analytically rather than chronologically. Similarly, I do not intend to offer any systematic account of Reformation theology – that has been quite adequately done elsewhere in a recent text by Bernard Reardon (7).

A survey of this kind is bound to be very provisional. Much of the material on which it is based is 'work in progress'. It consists either of general hypotheses which have yet to be subjected to rigorous investigation, or else of scattered case-studies from which it is difficult to generalise with complete confidence. Since every synthesis is bound to be a very personal matter, I have sought to make a virtue of necessity by presenting it as an interpretation of the German Reformation. In doing so I am conscious, as the reader should be, that it will be subject to amendment as Reformation studies progress further on the many fronts on which research is now being conducted. In what follows, I hope that where the argument is tentative or controversial, I have indicated the grounds on which it is based. The general bibliography serves this purpose, as well as providing a guide for more specialised further reading. For reasons of space, I have kept foreign language references to a minimum. I hope that many colleagues from whose work I have benefited greatly will forgive me if my debt to them is often tacitly rather than explicitly acknowledged.

Introduction to the
Second Edition

Sixteen years have passed since *The German Reformation* was first published. Given the amount of research that has been done since, there is now need for an additional commentary on recent developments. It is deeply regretted that this cannot be undertaken by the author himself, as Bob Scribner died on 29 January 1998, not long after taking up his appointment as Professor of Modern European Christianity at Harvard University. Instead, the editors of the series have asked me, as one of Bob's former students and a historian of the German Reformation, to provide an additional chapter synthesising the latest developments in the field along with a bibliography of recent works.

In keeping with the spirit of the first edition, the supplementary chapter is a synthesis of work in progress. The original lines of enquiry have been followed up, and in general the entire analysis remains true to the initial design, moving through the various themes raised in the seven chapters. At the same time, however, many of the research concerns that have evolved since 1986 have been integrated into the discussion, with a list of associated literature in the supplementary bibliography at the end of the book. Part of Bob Scribner's lasting legacy to Reformation studies was his ability to draw on a broad range of theories, disciplines and concepts and use them to bring aspects of the past to life. Quite often that meant returning to the details of local history or focusing on the unusual features of an image or a text in the search for new ways to think about the Reformation. And quite often that meant that work was always being revised and reformulated, always in progress.

In its way, the supplementary chapter attempts to do just that, to bring together a fairly wide range of related literature, much of it in the form of case studies and unexamined hypotheses, in the hope that it will incite interest and encourage the reader to think in different ways about the German Reformation. In this, as well, the chapter hopes to emulate the spirit of the original book, just as it hopes to do justice to the historical imagination of its author. He is greatly missed.

C. Scott Dixon, 2002

A Note on References

References are cited throughout in brackets according to the numbering in the select bibliography, with page references where necessary indicated by a colon after the bibliography number. Titles referred to in the supplementary chapter are numbered in bold and listed in the supplementary bibliography.

1   Some Reformation Myths

For most of us, the Reformation is 'Luther's Reformation', a massive response among the German people to a new faith proclaimed by Martin Luther and centred in Wittenberg. It is common to regard it as having begun in 1517, when Luther allegedly posted his 95 Theses on the door of the Castle Church in Wittenberg. Despite much scholarly debate, it remains uncertain whether the theses were ever posted; the real significance of the alleged incident resides in the fact that much later in the sixteenth century a myth was created that this was how 'the Reformation' began. This myth is typical of a number of myths about the Reformation. It involves a teleological view of history, an arrangement from hindsight of the course of events into an inevitable pattern, in which no other outcome is envisaged than 'the Reformation' as later ages understood it.

This point was made as long ago as 1965 by the church historian Bernd Moeller, who criticised excessive concentration on Luther and his theology, without proper regard for historical context. 'To caricature the common description, Luther generally appears as a great sage, a kind of spiritual colossus, who attains his Reformation breakthrough, draws the broad consequences, and then drags people with him as he strides through history handing out his truths right and left' (14: 13). Thus, as soon as Luther's ideas are promulgated, 'the Reformation' is in existence. It is then only a matter of people being 'won over to' or 'adhering to' this fully formed phenomenon. Historians then speak of 'popular support for the Reformation', without reflecting that 'the Reformation' did not yet exist, that it was a long drawn-out process of complex historical interrelations. Other reformers are then assessed against Luther as a standard, as

1

though they should have become (in Moeller's phrase) 'little Luthers'. Where they failed to measure up, they were denigrated or dismissed as insignificant.

Many historians have heeded Moeller's call to situate the Reformation more fully in its 'vital context', but the recent celebrations of the quincentenary of Luther's birth showed that just as many have ignored it. The view that the Reformation was the work of Luther alone, and that he was one of the heroes of history is still strong. This kind of mythological view of history has recently been joined by another, more secular interpretation. This seeks to find in the Reformation the beginnings of 'modernisation'. Influenced by Max Weber's idea that the Reformation introduces an ethical-rational approach to religion which had affinities with the 'spirit of capitalism', several historians perceive in the religious reform of the sixteenth century the conceptual basis, and sometimes even some practical antecedents, of the industrial societies that grew up from the mid-eighteenth century (see 12 for further discussion). This 'modernisation' view is a revived form of the whig interpretation of history, which sees history as part of an inevitable onward march of 'progress'. It shares much with the older church historical view of Luther, which sees him as 'the first modern man' and the forerunner of 'modern' freedoms.

How can we escape from this kind of myth-making about the Reformation? One important way is to set aside any kind of teleological perspective, to refuse to read history backwards with the view that the outcome of the religious upheavals of the sixteenth century was inevitable, or that what was successful was somehow better than that which failed. Here we face great difficulty, for the very words we use about the Reformation are the bearers of the myth, especially the term 'Reformation'. Luther never used it to refer to the events in which he was involved, and contemporary usage of the word was quite different from that of historians now. The term 'Reformation' to describe a historical period and a phase in church history did not appear until the seventeenth century, when it was used in polemical debates about whether Luther or Calvin had done more for the 'restoration of the church'. At the end of the seventeenth

2

century, Veit Ludwig von Seckendorf used it in a history of Lutheranism, but in a very narrow way which ignored other varieties of reformed belief. He meant by it *Luther's* criticism of the church, *Luther's* activities and *Luther's* creation of a new church. He therefore set the period of 'the Reformation' as coterminous with Luther's lifespan (1483–1546). In the eighteenth century, 'the Reformation' was given its mythological beginning in 1517, but assigned the *political* end-date of 1555, the year of the Peace of Augsburg. This settlement recognised only Lutheranism and Catholicism as approved religions within the Holy Roman Empire, but ignored other variants of 'evangelical Christianity' (15). 'The Reformation' thus became largely identical with Lutheranism, and the usage was finally enshrined by Leopold von Ranke in the 1830s, in a half-idealist, nationalist interpretation which has been normative down to our own day.

Other words have also been pressed into the service of this mythology: Lutheran, Calvinist, Protestant – all of which had different overtones in the sixteenth century. 'Lutheran' was first used as a term of abuse intended to smear Luther and his supporters as founders of a new sect. Luther never used it of his followers, and the term they most commonly used of themselves was at first 'Martinists', but then increasingly 'evangelical Christians'. The term 'Calvinist' was similarly a term of abuse first used between 1548 and 1553; those so labelled preferred to call themselves 'evangelical reformed Christians'. Only much later were these words adopted to describe the institutionalised forms of religion we now associate with them (15).

The term 'Protestant' had an equally limited frame of reference. It was originally a *political* term, referring to those estates of the Holy Roman Empire who objected in 1529 to the abrogation of the 1526 Recess of Speyer. This Recess was an ambiguous statement used by many secular authorities to legitimise religious innovation within their territories. When the political and constitutional protest of 1529 was given a doctrinal basis in 1530 by the Confession of Augsburg, it represented neither the full range of those who dissented from orthodox Catholicism, nor was it the result of any popular consensus. The Confession of Augsburg was something

3

of a politico-religious centaur, a theological statement worked out under diplomatic and political pressure to meet the demands of a political situation. It was a statement from which many 'evangelical Christians' dissented, and was to cause continuing dissension within their ranks. Whatever it was, 'the Reformation' was far broader and more complex than 'Protestantism' based on the Confession of Augsburg.

This is no idle quibble about mere words, since words with such specialised meanings are often the shorthand expression of ideology and myth. The notion that 'the Reformation' and 'Protestantism' sprang fully formed from the head of Luther was an important part of the self-legitimation of confessional churches in the nineteenth and twentieth centuries. To break away from such ideology, it is necessary to situate the religious events of the sixteenth century carefully in their historical context. Let us look at the sixteenth-century understanding of 'reformation'. The Latin word *reformatio* had three uses at that time. It meant a new legal code or set of statutes, as in the 'Reformation of the Imperial City of Nuremberg' of 1484. It also meant the restructuring of a university study curriculum (the sense in which Luther most commonly used it). Its third usage was religious, meaning internal reform of the church, a usage current throughout the fifteenth century, and best rendered in English by the word 'reform'.

The contemporary usage of *reformatio* was laden with overtones of popular belief. It would occur through a decisive intervention of God in human history, bringing about a 'great change' in the state of the world. This 'great change' had utopian and apocalyptic features, for it would inaugurate either a new age of the world, an 'age of the Spirit', or even perhaps the Last Days themselves, as foretold in the Book of Revelation. It would be announced by a *reformator*, a holy man or prophet sent by God as the instrument of this change. Luther's central role in the movements of religious reform that arose after 1520 can be traced in great part to the fact that he was identified with this figure. He was not seen just as a man with a remarkable new theology founded on his understanding of St Paul's notion of 'justification'. Onto him were also projected very traditional ideas about

4

the expected *reformator*, the holy man, the prophet, the saint sent by God. This understanding of Luther's 'mission' became a constituent part of Lutheran interpretations of the reform movements until at least the eighteenth century. Luther was a saint and a prophet, sent by God to 'reveal the Word' to his own age (23, 34, 35, 35a). Luther's contemporaries did not, however, see the whole process of 'reform' as dependent on him alone. Many other persons were singled out as sharing in this work: Erasmus, Karlstadt, Ulrich von Hutten, Zwingli, Melanchthon, Eberlin von Günzburg, to name only some of the more prominent. Nor was Wittenberg the only centre of renewal: alongside it contemporaries cited Zwickau, Erfurt, Strasbourg, Nuremberg and Zurich. The beginnings of religious reform were poly-centric and many-stranded. Confessional historiography has vastly distorted the full complexity of the 'age of reform', as it should more correctly be called (4). The ideological label 'the Reformation' has become too embedded as a description of a historical period for us to be able to dispense with it completely, but at least we can begin to mean by it a complex, extended historical process, going well beyond the endeav-ours of one man or one tendency, and involving social, political and wider religious issues.

2 Religion and Reform

Historians have always believed that an understanding of the religious dimensions of the Reformation could be found in the 'state of religion' of the age preceding it. Exactly what that 'state of religion' was, however, has been a matter of controversy, with at least four different analyses of its nature.

(1) There was a *profound religious malaise* in the century before the Reformation (22). This view seems to be confirmed by a broad range of fifteenth-century literature criticising religious abuses and failings, as well as by the criticisms of the sixteenth-century reformers. There is also evidence of low levels of church attendance, infrequent practice of the Sacraments and poor knowledge of the faith (20, 27).

(2) There was a *strong sense of devotion to the church and a powerful revival of piety* for at least two generations before the Reformation (25). In support of this thesis one can point to the growth of interest in mysticism and asceticism, to movements of lay piety such as the *Devotio moderna*, to the popularity of lay confraternities, to an increase in mass endowments, to a steady stream of devotional literature produced by the new art of printing, to new religious cults such as that of St Anne or the Rosary, and to a considerable revival of preaching.

(3) The problem was *not too little religion, but too much* (30). The demands of religious observance had become a spiritual burden, creating anxiety where religious comfort was sought. This was certainly the view held by Luther, who spoke of his own repeated attempts to

7

find consolation in the confessional, only to find that its rigours further ensnared his conscience, instead of easing it.

We should be cautious about accepting any of these three assessments as adequate versions of the real state of religion before the Reformation. Those based on the testimony of sixteenth-century reformers are especially suspect, since they could hardly be expected to portray in a favourable light a religious system they had so vehemently rejected. Sometimes historians have concentrated too much on formal standards of religious practice, for example, mass attendance or religious endowments, without asking how they might be related to the role of religion in everyday life. Sometimes they have examined only small segments of society, without asking how representative these were of the population as a whole. Lay confraternities, for example, were common enough in towns, but the vast mass of the rural population seem rarely to have participated in them to the same degree. The *Devotio moderna* involved only a tiny number of people; it was certainly influential with some intellectuals and churchmen, but it was far from representative of pre-Reformation religion. Nor were Luther's spiritual struggles typical of the everyday religious experience of ordinary layfolk, who had little cause to find the confessional burdensome, since most attended only once a year in fulfilment of their Easter duty. Luther's difficulties were more typical of a monastic piety based on spiritual athleticism, something which few layfolk either experienced or aspired to.

(4) *'Christian Europe' of the middle ages was hardly christian at all* (20). There was not just a low level of practice of Christianity, but a poor understanding of the fundamentals of Christian belief. All that had been achieved among the masses was to lay a thin veneer of Christianity over essentially pagan belief and practice, especially belief in a magical world of animism, spirits and demonic forces. The Reformation was part of

8

a long-term attempt to 'christianise' the masses, which began in the fifteenth century, and continued in what became the Reformation and Counter-Reformation. This at least broadens the enquiry beyond the study of small segments of the society, and asks questions about religion as believed and practised by the broadest mass of the population. Although much of the work associated with this approach has been conducted for France rather than Germany, there does seem to be something to be said for it, as we shall see later. However, there is also good evidence that 'christianisation' was more deep-rooted than it concedes. This can be seen in the extent to which the Bible permeated all levels of European culture, as well as the importance of Christian liturgy for popular life of the time (33, 136).

All four of these approaches rest on a number of implicit value judgments about what constitutes 'good' and 'bad' religion, against which the *quality* of pre-Reformation religious life is then assessed. In what has remained a very influential book, Johan Huizinga wrote in 1924 of late-medieval religion as having a decayed sensibility which reduced the religious to a matter of sense impressions, over-heated emotions and a shallowly visual perception of the sacred (22). Many recent historians follow the same path with a critique of what they regard as the 'inadequate' religion of the later middle ages. They contrast 'external' religion to 'true inward piety', 'oversimplified' and 'vulgarised' religion to 'tranquil spirituality'. In this tone, much of pre-Reformation religion is labelled as 'superstitious', implying that it was inferior and unacceptable (4, 27, 30). Such views merely accept the value judgments of sixteenth-century religious reformers, that theirs was a 'superior' form of religion, while what they attempted to reform was erroneous, indeed diabolically perverse.

How might we gain a better understanding of pre-Reformation religion? First, we should cease viewing it through the eyes of the reformers, and describe it in its own right. We could, for example, treat it as a 'religious culture' with different 'modes of religious experience', without making too many value judgments about the quality of that experience. We could then seek to pinpoint how it may have been changed or modified by the attempts at religious reform in the sixteenth century. Excellent examples of this approach can be found in recent work by Natalie Davis (5), Euan Cameron (131) and William A. Christian (18–19). Let us sketch out briefly some salient features identified through this approach.

The most fundamental belief was that the natural world was dependent on sacred power for its sustenance and well-being. Christianity asserted that God was the only supernatural being who sustained creation, but people of that age accepted the activity of numerous other beings who could wield supernatural power – the Devil, spirits both angelic and demonic, and numerous 'holy' persons who were believed to possess sacred power. This last group included not just the saints of Christian tradition, but also popular healers, magicians, 'cunning folk' and local and legendary 'holy folk'. This was a *sacramental* view of religion, one in which the sacred was manifested in and through the material world. Sacred beings could pass on their power to other persons, places or things by sympathy. Places where sacred persons appeared, things with which they came into contact became sacred themselves. This was especially true of the material remains of the saints and of their shrines (3, 18–19, 32).

As an institution with a Christian world-view, the church tried to 'christianise' such beliefs in two ways. It tried to claim a monopoly of sacred power for itself, exercised through its ordained priesthood; and it tried to police, and if necessary outlaw, others who disputed that claim. Lay folk who attempted to preach, those who professed to have had visions or to have worked miracles, popular prophets and holy folk, and especially the cults of local saints and their relics all came under the official scrutiny of the church before they were either approved (and so controlled) or rejected. Means of access to sacred power which the church regarded as unacceptable were condemned as 'superstitious' or magical, and were held to achieve their efficacy through the power of demons or the Devil. The church claimed, in any case, a superior power over these demonic and diabolic beings, especially through its ability to exorcise them through the use of ritual formulae. The struggle between the church and 'superstition' or magic, epitomised in the contest of priest and magician as rival practitioners of sacred power, reached its peak in the attack on witchcraft during the fifteenth century, when popular magic was stigmatised as a blasphemous pact with the Devil, punishable in the last resort by loss of life.

The church saw its primary role, of course, in preparing people for 'salvation', for the 'next life'. It offered in the Sacraments a number of means which guaranteed 'holiness' or an acceptable state for salvation. The Sacraments sanctified the individual believer and all of his or her relationships at key points throughout the life-cycle: at birth (Baptism), the attainment of adulthood (Confirmation), reproduction (Matrimony) and death (Extreme Unction, or the Last Rites). As manifestations of sacred power, in the Christian view of them, manifestations of God's saving grace, they were automatically effective. Alongside them, the church offered a number of other means of holiness, the so-called Sacramentals. These originated in blessings and exorcisms through which the church tried to repel the demonic forces present in the world, in order to make it safe for human use and able to contribute to human salvation.

This was the church's answer to the appeal of popular magic, since the Sacramentals all involved some form of instrumental application of sacred power for human daily needs. They involved exorcisms and blessings, such as weather blessings intended to still storms, or prayers to beseech protection over cattle and crops, house and hearth. There were also blessed objects, such as candles, palms, salt and water, which could be taken away and used as the individual desired. Almost all the Sacramentals met the needs of an agrarian society coping with the perils of daily life: sickness in humans and animals, threats to crops from weather or pests, poor fertility of land or beasts. In theory, the Sacramentals were aids to piety, a way of invoking God's protection over body and soul, yet popular usage made them rather a form of Christian magic, treating them as though they were magically

11

efficacious (33). The church guaranteed automatic efficacy only for the Sacraments, although the Sacramentals probably replaced them in religious importance, largely because of the frequency of their use. Sacraments were infrequent, Sacramentals a matter of daily use.

The only Sacrament which was a matter of daily experience was the Eucharist, involving the transformation of bread and wine into the body and blood of Christ, according to the doctrine of Transsubstantiation, each time the Mass was celebrated. This was the most powerful of all manifestations of the sacred – God himself was physically present in the elements of the wafer-bread and the wine. It is not surprising that the Eucharist became the central object of popular belief and devotion, as well as a major point of dispute between the church and the reformers. In the Eucharist was embodied the entire essence of the sacramental and magical world, as well as the church's claims to be able to control it.

At the end of the fifteenth century, the church was attempting to tighten this control in two ways. It began to police more carefully alternative forms of access to the sacred, with reforms aimed at 'superstitious' religion and a vigorous attack on popular magic (3). It also began to improve the quality of the clergy, to 'professionalise' them. Both steps may have been seen as an affront to ordinary layfolk, who showed a growing hostility to the church and the clergy. They resented the increasing tendency of church and clergy to charge for the sacred services they provided over and above what most people could afford to pay. This was not just an economic but also a religious grievance – it involved the serious sin of simony: the buying or selling of sacred things (Acts 8; 18–19). Not unrelated to this was the hostility of the laity to what they saw as the increasing disparity between what the clergy professed to be and what they were. The church provided one assured route to salvation through a life said to be unfailingly pleasing to God, the 'religious life' in a monastic order. This seemed to divide people into two classes, those apparently sure of salvation and those not. Since the behaviour of the regular clergy frequently left much to be desired, it is not surprising that lay people were struck with a sense of the injustice of the situation. Anticlericalism expressed a sense of lay outrage against clerical hypocrisy among both the regular and the secular clergy.

Increasingly, the laity began to find ways to the sacred that either bypassed the clergy or minimised their control. Lay confraternities were one such means; another was to subject the clergy to closer lay supervision, although this was most successful in towns. There were attempts to adapt the religious life of monastic communities to lay circumstances, through lay communities or through exercises of piety modelled on those of the monastic orders. People turned to private and group devotions, such as the Rosary or contemplation of the sufferings of Christ or the Virgin. They also looked for the direct intervention of the divine, usually in the form of some supernatural apparition, or in the appearance of a new holy man and prophet. The foremost example of the last, which aroused a mass outbreak of religious enthusiasm, was the appearance of the Drummer of Niklashausen in 1476. Some were inspired by the vision of the 'new age of the Spirit' or by 'visions of the End' (24, 31). Both were to be announced by the coming of a holy man who would chastise the clergy and reform the church. As public attention began to focus on Luther around 1520, he was quickly identified as that man, not least because he seemed to attack the clergy and their greed.

Luther was both a man of his age and a very atypical figure. A man of deep religious concerns, sincerely worried about his salvation, he was however a trained theologian and humanist, immersed in biblical, theological and classical sources. He sought an answer to his personal dilemma in study of the Bible, and although he found his release in a deep personal insight, it was the response of an intellectual, resting on a complex understanding of a Pauline-Augustinian theology. His central perception was that salvation had been achieved once and for all by Christ's death and was therefore unconditional. His awareness that God gave grace freely and unconditionally in this way, allied with his pessimistic belief in the minimal role of human beings in contributing to their own salvation led him to stress that salvation depended only on a response in faith to God's call to salvation, a response which the individual Christian was free to make, but which

13

was forced upon him or her by the overpowering grace of God (17).

By 1520 Luther's insight was more a religious perception than a systematic theological construction, and he had not worked out fully or clearly many of its implications. Those that he did work out and communicate to a wider audience were certainly of radical importance. His view of salvation challenged the basis of the church as it then was, and many of its practices. Luther also saw it as bringing an extraordinary amount of freedom to the practice of religious belief (although for many people less scrupulous than Luther, that freedom already existed). He also emphasised the centrality of the Word of God in the Bible as the main means of encountering and experiencing faith. These views were so strongly held and expressed that they blotted out, or at least subordinated a great deal of what was traditional in Luther's mentality – as they have been blotted out of the awareness of many historians subsequently. It is worth stressing some of them here, in order to emphasise how far Luther remained a child of his own age.

Luther's religious perceptions were almost certainly influenced by the strong scepticism felt by many of his generation about the church's claims to manipulate sacred power, an unease which was increasingly directed against the doctrine of Transsubstantiation. That scepticism was in turn influenced by strong currents of nominalism, the late-medieval philosophy which denied the reality of universals, emphasised the mysteriousness and arbitrariness of God, and placed great weight on the powers of human reason. One consequence of this belief was to undermine belief in a magical and wholly sacramental world. As Heiko Oberman has shown, nominalism employed a rational scepticism about the power of magic to influence the natural world, combined with a belief in the absolute power of God so strong that it did not allow for the effective activity of any intermediate sacred being (29). This not only destroyed belief in magic, the manipulation of sacred power by humans; it also destroyed belief in Sacramentals, and even in the Sacraments themselves.

Luther followed this intellectual path, which could have led logically to what Max Weber called the 'disenchantment

14

of the world', the removal of all intermediate causes between God and the laws of nature. But neither the nominalists nor Luther (who was anything but a logical thinker) followed the logic to its conclusion. Here we may see the limits of nominalist influence on Luther, who found a more enduring influence in the Bible, especially in the Epistles of St Paul. And since such things were mentioned in the Bible, Luther and many of his followers, those who eventually became Protestants, continued to believe in the Devil, demons and angels, spirits, ghosts and poltergeists.

Luther also believed strongly in the imminence of the Last Days, or at least in the 'great change' of the world, and came to see himself as the long-foretold divinely ordained prophet who was to announce it (35). He shared the popular belief in the presence and activity of the Antichrist, the figure with whom he so successfully identified the papacy (45). As Oberman has recently shown, Luther's sense of religious struggle was shaped by the very medieval idea of the battle between God and the Devil, with a great cosmic showdown occurring in his own day, around the reform movement in which he was involved (28). Thus, a great deal of Lutheran theology was to be devoted to explaining the paradox that although God was so absolute in the world as to render Sacraments and Sacramentals in the old sense useless and blasphemous, the Devil still seemed to have power over the world, magic still appeared possible, and exorcism and other prayer against the Devil was still necessary. One of the most important recent contributions to Reformation studies has pointed to the limited impact of Reformation ideas, especially in the countryside (119). Part of the limitation can perhaps be found in the inability of reformed ideas to change magical perceptions of the world, something to which the strong reformed belief in the power of the Devil can only have contributed.

Luther was not the only person of his day to reject a sacramental, magical world-view. The same was done not only by many intellectuals, but also by radical religious thinkers and small pockets of religious dissenters (6, 131). Nor was he the only person to discover that salvation came through reliance on God alone, and to evolve a theology based upon St Paul

15

and St Augustine. Luther was not as unique as subsequent church history has made him out to be. That the movement that sprang up in response to the 'Luther affair' in the early 1520s created a new church cannot be explained either by reliance on Luther himself, or by theological factors alone. Indeed, rather than carrying all before it, what came to be called Lutheranism can be said to have been very limited in its impact. This is a theme to be pursued in later chapters.

3 The Reformation as an Evangelical Movement

For some time now it has been common for scholars of the Reformation to speak of it as an 'evangelical movement'. The term captures the tone of the upsurge of religious enthusiasm that swept through Germany in the early 1520s. In its broadest manifestations, it was a movement of biblical renewal. Many felt that the genuine Christian message, the 'pure Word of God' as it was recorded in the Bible, had been rediscovered after it had lain hidden or obscured for many generations. Religious fervour was certainly the dominant characteristic of this movement. For those involved, the biblical revival offered a new meaning to many areas of life, a changed perspective of their relationship to God and the world. An important feature of the movement was the conviction that religious revival was not just the work of mere human beings, but the result of a direct intervention of God into human history, the work of the Holy Spirit. Many, including Luther, saw this as a decisive sign of the imminence of the Last Days. The catchword of this movement was 'the Gospel' or 'the Word of God': one was either for the Gospel or against it, one agreed to 'stand by the Gospel' and to 'uphold the pure Word of God'.

Beyond its catchwords, what was the message of this movement? It is traditional to associate it with the doctrines of Luther, and these certainly played a prominent role, not least because of the status accorded him as a holy man and prophet, the expected *reformator*. However, the evangelical message was far more complex than the ideas of one man. It had both positive and negative elements. The negative elements drew on an endemic anticlericalism, the product of

17

a long history of lay disillusionment with the clergy (37–8, 53). The clergy were accused of hypocrisy, tyranny and deceit, of exploiting the religious needs of layfolk for personal gain, and of burdening them with unnecessary demands and exactions (29, 30). Priests and monks were stigmatised as 'enemies of the Gospel', as representatives of irreligion, who were likely to lead people to damnation rather than to salvation. The clergy were depicted as allies of the Devil; indeed, they were agents of the Antichrist, the ultimate personification of evil, who was now exposed as none other than the Pope, an alien power (in both a geographical and metaphysical sense), who was exploiting the German people for diabolical purposes (45).

The positive message stood in counterpoint to the negative: the laity no longer needed the clergy for salvation, since each Christian was free to find salvation through a direct encounter with God in the Bible. This encounter occurred in two ways: through reading the Bible, and through hearing the Word preached. The latter provided the main slogan of the movement, the demand for the preaching of the 'pure Word of God' (50). One aspect of this message gave it a broader thrust than it would have had if it had been confined to purely religious ideas. The Word was seen not just as a way to salvation, but as a guide for life in the world. The Gospel provided an ethical standard against which to measure secular life, so that a good deal of social grievance was immediately involved in the content of the message. The age of early capitalism and the backwash of the late medieval crisis of agrarian feudalism gave rise to innumerable social conflicts and struggles over social justice. Now matters long complained of as unjust were given a final stamp of unacceptability by being shown to be contrary to the Word of God. This transition was the more easily made since the clergy, with their legal and economic privileges, were regarded as a major cause of social grievance (38, 134).

To appreciate the nature and extent of the evangelical movement, it is therefore important to understand that it combined several elements in its message: an attack on the state of the church, as well as on the state of society; a message about the way to salvation, and a message about how to improve life in this world. There was another essential element: this message was directed at ordinary lay Christians. Indeed, in its initial propaganda, the ordinary lay Christian was idealised as the chief supporter of the Gospel and of its recovery in all its purity. An idealised image of this lay Christian was created by identifying him with the 'common man', a stock term used to designate the ordinary town- or country-dweller. The 'common man' was as good a Christian as, or even better than, the professional men of religion, the priests and monks; he was more learned in the Word than the scholar, for he could better understand it and expound its religious message (36). The 'common man' found his archetypal representation in the figure of Karsthans, the 'evangelical peasant', in ragged breeches and boots, shouldering his hoe or threshing-flail in defence of the Gospel (1, 30, 45). It is interesting that this idealised figure of the 'ordinary Christian' was male: there were virtually no stereotyped ideals presented for imitation by women interested in evangelical ideas! But Karsthans was a fictitious figure entirely, for the majority of the movement's leaders were clergymen, and initially most of its followers were townsmen, rather than peasants (144). However, for four or five years this image encouraged the widest possible dissemination of the evangelical message. In these years, there seemed to be no barriers to its success.

The speed with which the movement spread certainly convinced its adherents that they were taking part in the direct work of God. Much has been made of the role of printing in this rapid dissemination. Luther saw it as 'God's highest and extremest act of grace, whereby the business of the Gospel is driven forward', and many historians of our own day echo this judgment (39, 41, 51). Printing created a new reading public, who seized eagerly on the reformers' ideas to form a large-scale 'public opinion', which in turn served to spread the movement on a mass scale (15). This was certainly assisted by the many printers who became emphatic supporters of the new ideas (40). However, some caution is necessary before accepting this view without reservation. Literacy was very low in sixteenth-century Germany, and perhaps only 4 or 5 per cent of the population could

19

read. It was certainly widespread in towns. In areas of urban concentration, such as south-west Germany, where no one was more than a few miles from a town, and so from its educational and cultural influence, it may even have been common for countryfolk as well. However, the reading public may have comprised no more than 400 000 individuals in a total estimated population of sixteen million. It has been estimated that between 1517 and 1520 some 300 000 copies of Luther's various writings were published, enough for every reader to own at least one copy of a work by Luther, assuming that no one bought more than one, and that some copies were passed around. Even so, only 2.3 per cent of the population, or one person in forty-three, would have encountered Luther's ideas in this way.

In fact, the spread of evangelical ideas depended as much on forms of oral communication as it did on printing. Sixteenth-century Germany was still predominantly an oral culture, in which information was passed on by word of mouth through personal contacts. Printing did create the possibility of a large-scale, impersonal reading public, but this was nothing like a modern 'public opinion'. Perhaps it could more validly be said that printing created 'opinion leaders', people who had read of the new ideas, and were able to pass them on further by word of mouth (46). However, it seems fairly certain that the real mass dissemination of ideas took place orally, not through the printed word; and the most powerful oral means of dissemination was the sermon. More than anything else, the evangelical movement was a powerful preaching revival. It was the preaching and hearing of the Word that formed its constituent element (50).

The foundations of this preaching revival were laid well before Luther ever appeared on the public scene. The desire for more and improved preaching had led to a wave of lay-funded preacherships in Germany in the two generations before 1520. We can find these being established in both urban and rural parts of Thuringia, Bavaria and Wurttemberg, with as many as 42 being founded in the last territory. Revivalist preachers were exceptionally popular during the fifteenth and the early sixteenth century, especially those with the skills of a John Capistrano or a Geiler von Keysersberg.

It is significant that the popular prophetic literature awaited a preaching reformer, and that Luther was so quickly identified with this figure, being depicted not as a writer of theological tracts, but as a friar preaching the Word (45). Many of the preachers who initiated the evangelical movement of the 1520s held these funded preacherships: Steven Ozment has identified 23 such out of 42 towns where the new ideas spread (30).

This was an important factor in the preachers' advocacy of religious reform, for they were able to speak from the security of established positions. Their skill as preachers was probably related to two other aspects of the pre-1520 preaching revival. First, there had been a conscious attempt to improve the standard of preaching by providing handbooks for parish priests, containing either model sermons or collections of postils (expositions in German of the weekly Epistle and Gospel) as an aid to sermon composition. Second, many of the first preachers came from the mendicant orders, such as the Franciscans and the Augustinians, who had strong traditions of popular vernacular preaching.

The evangelical movement most commonly began through the pulpit, which had rightly been called the major mass medium of the age. The preachers were not wholly unprepared for this task. Many had received an initial impulse from humanism, whose importance for the biblical revival cannot be overestimated (42, 64). Erasmus advocated a biblical rather than a philosophical theology, based on restored texts of the Bible, and he also advised many of his followers to turn to preaching the pure Gospel. Much of the new preaching was regular preaching, at regular times from established preachers, but there was also much irregular preaching, which was found wherever wandering preachers sought to proclaim their newly awakened religious enthusiasm. These were mostly former monks or friars, sometimes priests dismissed from their posts for holding evangelical ideas. Less commonly they were laymen, and occasionally women turned to preaching, though this was very rare. Sometimes these preachers had been schoolmasters, half-clerical persons, since schoolmasters were usually in minor orders.

21

Irregular sermons were also marked by their informality of place. If no church was available for preaching, either because a preacher spontaneously decided to preach, or because he was denied access to a church, sermons were held in churchyards or under trees. Sebastian Froeschel was prevented from preaching in St John's church in Leipzig in 1523 because the provost had locked the doors, so his supporters simply set up a pulpit for him in the churchyard. In 1522 Johannes Zymler, a schoolmaster, preached from a window of his schoolhouse to a crowd gathered outside. Indeed, any preacher of any ability soon attracted crowds, initially enticed as much by the novelty value and newsworthiness of his sermons as by any knowledge of the content. Sometimes preaching occurred as 'hedgepreaching', sermons in private to small groups of fellow believers (44, 46–7).

This kind of preaching enabled the new ideas to bridge the cultural divide between town and country, and between literate and illiterate. Countryfolk heard the message from their pastor (in the few cases where rural clergy were inspired by the message), or else from a wandering preacher. Or they attended a sermon in a nearby market town, probably the most common way for the message to spread into the countryside. From the sermon, evangelical ideas were passed on by all the means open to oral communication. They were discussed at home, at the workplace, in inns, on the market square and in the street (46, 134). For the illiterate and semi-literate, there were also illustrated broadsheets, with skilfully drawn woodcut pictures, often with a rhyming text that could be sung or easily memorised (45). And as the evangelical movement gathered momentum, there were songs, ballads and hymns, intended both to spread the message further and to arouse solidarity among supporters (46).

The dissemination of the evangelical message in such varied forms explains a good deal of the diffuseness that quickly characterised it (144). Historians always stress the uniformity and authority of the printed word in creating a coherent movement around a well-defined body of religious doctrines. However, if we examine the way the new ideas spread orally, we see that it was far less defined, far less coherent. Personal discussion of ideas enabled people to make their own choices of the ideas they heard, to impose their own understanding on them, rendering the content of the message more diffuse and complex. This could be compensated for by the skill of the preacher, who might use rhetorical devices of repetition and recapitulation, and who sought to attract his audience back to hear further sermons, in which poorly understood points might be clarified or reinforced. Whether this was sufficient to create any uniformity of belief is uncertain. What is certain is that it created fervour and impatience for change.

Impatience for change was the dominant mood of the movement. It was this which produced a militancy of behaviour and engendered turbulence almost everywhere the movement appeared (44). Impatience was expressed through the form of direct action: most people inspired by the new ideas were not content simply to stop buying indulgences, to cease funding requiem masses or to give up attending the old religious services. They decided that they must act decisively to stop the clergy continuing in their old course. This may have had many emotional components. It was doubtless fired by the long-standing discontent with the church and the clergy, and by anger at having been misled over religion in the past. There was also a sense that the old practices, as people now understood them, were irreligious and that to continue with them was blasphemous, and might endanger the salvation of all. Some even feared physical danger: God might vent his anger against irreligion in this-worldly terms. The awareness that the 'great change' had at last arrived, that the Antichrist had been exposed, and that the great struggle had begun which presaged the Last Days, all undoubtedly played a part. The belief that such practices were the works of the Antichrist – for so they were represented by evangelical propaganda – certainly influenced the desire to be rid of them at once (45).

Propaganda played a part in arousing this militant impatience. It incited people to action on behalf of the Gospel, depicting with approval those who took violent steps against the old clergy and the old belief. The preachers themselves often gave the lead, if not always through their own militant actions, certainly through their violence of speech, Luther among them (89). They too incited their followers to militant behaviour in sermons, tracts and broadsheets. Such behaviour took the form of what one historian has called 'reformation through provocation' (49): disruption of the sermons of those who did not preach the 'pure Word of God', disturbance of church services, ceremonies and processions, personal abuse of the clergy, and attacks on their persons and property, ranging from jostling them in the street, singing ditties about them by night and day, smashing their windows, sometimes storming their houses, right through to mass expulsions of priests, monks and nuns. There were attacks on images and other cult objects, and other acts of what would today be called vandalism; and even acts of obscene exhibitionism, such as the man who exposed himself in St Ulrich's church in Augsburg in 1533, as a gesture of contempt for the traditional service being conducted there.

To sum up, the evangelical movement that emerged in Germany in the years 1520–24 was characterised by a combination of strong religious fervour, impatience, militancy and turbulence. Its strength can perhaps be found in the multiplicity and diffuseness of its message, in which people found themselves united in a consciousness of a common cause, the revival of the Gospel both as a means of salvation, and as a means of leading a just Christian life in this world. This common cause was embodied in a number of general catchwords and slogans, which disguised the diversity and complexity of ideas motivating it. However, this enabled it to expand into areas where someone as socially and politically conservative as Luther never dreamed it would go. Indeed, if the movement had remained within the limits to which Luther and others who thought like him sought to confine it, it might have remained as limited in its impact as earlier movements of religious reform. It attained wider significance because it quickly outran Luther's ideas, and achieved a near-revolutionary impetus of its own.

4 Social Location of the Reformation

We are now well accustomed to asking about the social composition of such movements of change, and this chapter will provide a brief sociology of the reform movement. To say that it found adherents among all social groups is an unhelpful truism. What we need to know for an adequate sociology is whether its adherents were drawn disproportionately from one social group or another, and whether there were significant differences in how each group understood its message. We should also examine any differences between leaders and followers, and whether there was any differential appeal in terms of age, gender, occupation or profession and wealth. We should also ask questions about different degrees of participation: were some people only lightly touched by its message, as opposed to more fervent adherents? Were different categories of adherents characterised by different forms of behaviour? Can we draw any significant distinction between active or passive adherents? At this stage of the research, it is difficult to provide firm answers to all these questions (see 55), but we now have enough case-studies to risk a crude sketch.

The prevailing view of the last twenty years has been that the reform movement found its most ready response in towns, especially among the imperial cities (those with no immediate overlord other than the Emperor). It was argued that they found in evangelical belief a religion conformable to their notion that salvation was a collective matter for the whole urban community, and that religious reform served to preserve its peace and unity (65). Because the imperial cities were concentrated in the south-west corner of Germany, the emphasis fell naturally enough on a 'south German Reformation', roughly the area south of the river Main (see esp. 137). However, the same characteristics have been identified in the towns of north and central Germany, in fact in most towns which possessed or aimed at autonomy in government. There has been a recent suggestion that the Hansa towns of north and north-west Germany experienced a different type of reform movement (83), but this 'Hansa city Reformation' has yet to be established as a distinctive type.

Research so far has been too unsystematic, concentrating either on large towns such as Nuremberg or Strasbourg, or on imperial cities, to the neglect of small towns under territorial rule (but see 70, 134). There were only around a dozen towns of the size of Nuremberg or Strasbourg, and only 65 imperial cities, so that most of our research energies have been devoted to perhaps no more than 80 of the 2000 or more towns in sixteenth-century Germany. The *typical* town had a population of between 500 and 2000, and was a farm town, more rural in its outlook than the term 'city' implies. However, even if we take all the towns of Germany together, they would account for no more than 10 per cent of the total population. If the reform movement was essentially an 'urban phenomenon', as most historians believe it to be (1, 51), it would have affected only a tiny proportion of the German people as a whole. This clearly underestimates the importance of the countryside, to which we shall return later.

If we concentrate on the movement within the towns, it is clear that response to its message was socially very varied. Even when an entire town committed itself to institutionalised reform, it would be a mistake to assume that all its inhabitants did so with the same enthusiasm or motives. The numerical bulk of support always appeared to come from the middling artisan classes, but these made up the bulk of any urban population, and artisans do not appear to have been over-represented among supporters of reform. Urban patricians were often under-represented, while well-to-do merchants sometimes appear in disproportionate numbers (44). It is difficult to generalise about individual professions, most of which turn up among evangelical Christians. There were wealthy trades such as goldsmiths, middling to wealthy such as furriers, and poorer trades such as shoemakers. Intellectuals and the professions seemed to take up the religious message with alacrity, especially those with humanist training, although in any really typical town there would have been only minute numbers of these. Printers, artists and woodcarvers all seemed eager for the new ideas, and not only because they stood to profit from the high demand for religious literature. Artists and woodcarvers actually stood to lose a great deal from reform, and after being attracted to the Gospel, many ceased producing traditional religious works. Weavers often appear as adherents of evangelical ideas, although they were a populous and radical trade. Sometimes smiths provided the kernel of support, as they did in Schwäbisch Gmünd, and in some towns an entire guild promoted reform, as the gardeners did in Strasbourg in 1523.

There has been considerable interest in the response of women (59, 62, 143) and the young (30), but the evidence adduced so far has been inconclusive. We can say little definite about the scale of adherence among women, except that they gave active support, but in considerably smaller numbers than men. It is unusual to find incidents such as that in Schlettstadt in Alsace, where in February 1525 numbers of women invaded a convent of Dominican nuns, in order to convince them of the error of their way of life and 'to turn them to the Gospel' (134: 69). This may only reflect the limited role allowed to women in the communal politics of the day, and their involvement may have been more frequently expressed in different ways we have yet to locate in the sources. For example, some Anabaptist sources show women influencing others and being influenced within the household as wives and domestic servants (46: 244). On the other hand, women sometimes stand out as the opponents of the new belief, for example in Ulm, where they continued to lead devotion to images after the introduction of reform in 1531. Some Ulm women even claimed to have had a miraculous vision in 1528, an event hushed up by the authorities because it was an embarrassment to their advocacy of reform.

The young often appear as the most active supporters of the new ideas (69), but this may be misleading. First, we might expect the young to be more militant and boisterous in opposition to the established order – the unruliness of students, apprentices and journeymen was a constant headache to authorities of the time. Second, demographic factors determined that the young made up a very great proportion of the society. Like artisans, if they turned out for reform in considerable numbers, it was because there were more of them to turn out.

The strongest response from a single occupational or professional group came from the clergy, especially the highly educated urban clergy. The rural clergy were less enthusiastic, shown convincingly by an enquiry among the rural clergy of Ulm in 1531, when only a handful of more than a hundred interviewed had any awareness of the issues of the reform, much less inclination to support it (1). Nonetheless, the clergy provided the bulk of the leaders of the reform movement, curious for a movement with such strong elements of anticlericalism. Study of a sample group of leading evangelical preachers shows that over three-quarters of them were members of the old clergy. Almost all were university educated, and over half had a higher degree (for purposes of comparison, less than 1 per cent of the total population ever attended university). The preachers were almost wholly from urban backgrounds, and a disproportionate number came from the urban upper classes (47). This clearly influenced their ability to get on with the ruling elites in the towns: often the success of reform depended on the degree of harmony between preachers and town rulers, or on the strength of personality of the preachers in influencing them (130, 137).

The lay leaders of reform were of different kinds (12, 15). Often they were influential persons in the community who attempted to use their social prestige to further reform (130). A petition presented to Duke George of Saxony in 1524 by 105 citizens of Leipzig, pleading for a preacher to proclaim the Word of God, was signed by 84 persons from the richest members of society (44). More important were town councillors and city mayors inclined to the new ideas.

They often constituted a pressure group within the town council pushing for reform, and indeed in a town such as Nuremberg, religious reform was instituted virtually at the initiative of the town council (30). Sometimes, where a single individual could establish a dominance in city politics his influence could be decisive in introducing reform, as in the cases of Adolarius Huttener in Erfurt (66) or Bernhard Besserer in Ulm (30). City secretaries were also important because of their access to the decision-making process, and because they were often trained lawyers able to give invaluable advice about the implications of reform. Lazarus Spengler of Nuremberg (60) and Jorg Vogeli of Constance (130) are well-known examples, but there were many more. The views of trained jurists were often decisive in weighing up the pros and cons of reform. Sometimes even evangelical jurists advised against it because of the political and economic dangers, as occurred in Augsburg (56, 57) and Regensburg in 1534 and Speyer in 1538 (67).

When we turn to the followers of the urban movement, it is difficult to go beyond reports of collective action, where guilds, parishes, the urban commune or even just large crowds of people demanded reform. In Basel, for example, over a dozen guilds were active in exerting pressure on the town council in 1529, while in Strasbourg both the gardeners' guild in 1523, and five of the nine parishes in 1524, demanded an evangelical preacher (30, 58, 134). In Memmingen, it was the organised city commune which in 1525 demanded religious reform from a reluctant council (11). Often these expressions of collective support were so entangled with urban politics that it is difficult to separate religious demands from social, economic and political grievances advanced at the same time (see Chapter 5).

We should certainly be wary of the referenda taken in over a dozen or more towns, which many historians cite as evidence of total popular support for reform. Even where they list by name the voters for and against, we must take account of what question was put to the voters, and how it was put. Usually only citizens could vote, who could be no more than a fifth of the population. In Ulm some 1600 guildsmen voted in November 1530, out of a total population of around

14 000. Often the question was put in guild assemblies or to a mass assembly, so that there was hardly a secret ballot, and the issue of reform was rarely put directly. Moreover, the question was often put only to men, as heads of households or as male citizens, so that it tells us nothing about that half of the population who were female. There is also the problem of what kind of real choice the referendum represented – often it could be no more than a legitimating mechanism for a decision already taken by the magistrates. The results may tell us little about who went along with the decision out of ignorance, indifference or fear, so that such votes are perhaps most useful to identify the determined opponents of reform. The Ulm referendum was a vote on whether to accept the Recess of the Diet of Augsburg (which reaffirmed the Edict of Worms condemning Luther). It was indeed clear to many guildsmen that they were voting to 'stand by the Gospel', but it is interesting that 262 voted against, around 16 per cent of the voters. With such a sizeable group of determined opponents of reform, it is not surprising that we find a small and persistent group of Ulmers who remained loyal to the old faith (on these votes, 139: 122–3).

Nonetheless, in many places there is evidence of a very broad base of support for evangelical ideas, attested by the large numbers who often turned out to hear sermons. In Nuremberg, Diepold Beringer, the so-called Peasant of Woehrd, was reported to have had an audience of thousands, and in Kitzingen he was said to have preached to 8000 (11). (We are not told how he was audible to so many!) Many in his audience were countryfolk, doubtless lured by the appeal of a 'preaching peasant' who seemed learned in the Bible (though Beringer was a fraud: he was an ex-monk and a trained theologian, not an illiterate man suddenly enlightened by the Word!). Such numbers reflect rural as well as urban interest in the Gospel, and when the first reformed German mass was held in Reutlingen in 1524, great crowds streamed into the town from surrounding districts (130). It seems undeniable that it was rural, rather than urban support which turned the reform movement into a *mass* movement, but it is difficult to break rural communities down into their component social parts as we are able to do in the towns. Sometimes the only evidence we have of rural interest is in the form of requests for a preacher, or in the appearance of a local priest who turned to 'preaching the Gospel' (see 134 for some of the best evidence cited in recent work).

The most striking hypothesis advanced to date has been that of Peter Blickle (36), who emphasises the propaganda appeal made to the 'common man' as the ideal Christian. The notion of the 'common man', referring to the lower orders of town and country, served as a bridge between the two social milieus. The ideas of Christian liberty and of the Word of God as an infallible standard of Christian life in the world provided such common people with a powerful weapon of protest. They challenged the basis of existing society, and justified revolt against it, developing a religiously founded 'mentality of resistance' (134, and see Chapter 5). As embodied in the Twelve Articles, the main manifesto of the peasant rebels of 1524–26, which was spread and accepted throughout Germany, these ideas turned the evangelical movement into a biblically legitimated revolution.

If Blickle is right, then there was a mass popular reception of evangelical ideas among the peasantry, and we can certainly speak of the German Peasants' War as an evangelical–social movement. However, it is also possible that many of the statements expressing radical biblicism were written into peasant manifestoes by leaders from the educated urban elite (61). We can neither prove nor disprove Blickle's hypothesis until we have more studies about how the new ideas were received in the countryside. So far we have only one recent work which pursues the question adequately, Franziska Conrad's investigation of the reception of evangelical ideas in the Alsace countryside (134).

Conrad finds that the peasants were genuinely inspired by the new preaching, but what can be reconstructed of their understanding of the 'evangelical message' shows that they had little or no interest in Luther's complex understanding of 'justification', and were most responsive to the communitarian religious views advanced by Martin Bucer in Strasbourg. They regarded the Gospel as a means of salvation which overturned the claims of the old church, but merged this into their practical concerns with an ethical shaping of Christian life and the achievement of a just society. This makes their religious outlook appear close to a traditional 'works righteousness' informed by a radical evangelism.

After the defeat of the Peasants' War, the desire for 'evangelical preaching' remained strong among the Alsatian peasantry, but the determination of Catholic authorities not to concede it, and the caution of reformed authorities about being involved in renewed social upheaval led to a loss of religious fervour. By the 1540s the complaint was of peasant indifference to reform, rather than enthusiasm for it. This echoes the view of many historians that there was rather less enthusiasm for evangelical ideas in rural areas after 1525. Perhaps such ideas had not struck very deep roots in the peasantry, or the peasants were moved to abandon their initial interest out of disillusionment with the failure of Luther and other prominent reformers to support their call for social justice on the basis of the Word of God.

Here the Zurich countryside was perhaps typical. Their preachers had told them that if they would commit their lives and goods in support of the Gospel, their new-won evangelical freedom would be to their advantage. Accordingly, the peasantry applied to their overlords in the city of Zurich for remission of the tithe, since this was clearly not grounded in the Word. However, they were told that although the Gospel did not command giving the tithe, it also did not command not giving it, and it should be paid out of Christian love. The preacher Johannes Stumpf later recorded how little pleased the peasants were with this reply: 'many came to a great hatred of the preachers, where before they would have bitten off their feet for the Gospel'.

The nobility have also been relatively neglected because of the interest lavished on the towns, but they seemed to show an initial enthusiasm for reform, followed by a more cautious attitude (71, 130). It has been argued that the evangelical movement represented an anti-noble form of religion (32), but many minor noblemen adopted the cause of the Gospel eagerly from the beginning. The overall pattern of response was patchy, with the most concentrated adherence coming from the imperial knights in the Rhineland and Franconia, led by the charismatic figures of Ulrich von Hutten, Franz von Sickingen and Hartmut von Cronberg. The defeat of the Knights' Revolt of 1523 perhaps helped to discredit some of this fervour among the nobility, especially Hutten's passionate call for an anticlerical war to root out all priests and papists.

In the period up to 1555 there seems to be no clear pattern of noble allegiance, although it is clear that the nobility as a group stood to lose more from a thoroughgoing reform of the church than any other social class, since church offices provided one of their major forms of family income. These considerations certainly played a role in the introduction of the reforms in Hesse, where Landgrave Philip was unwilling to confiscate church properties for fear of reaction by his nobles (84).

After 1555 most minor nobles found themselves bound by the terms of the Peace of Augsburg, which stipulated that subjects should adopt the same religion as their rulers, a provision from which the lesser nobility were not exempt. Nonetheless, the nobility in many places were able to adopt a religious allegiance contrary to that of their territorial lord, which suggests that religion had become another bargaining counter in the complex game of territorial politics. The most notable example of such noble religious dissidence was in the Habsburg lands in Austria and the Steiermark, where noble support for reform was strong from the early 1520s (13, 71). Yet the most influential role played by the nobility was probably that in Saxony, where they were employed as local officials and administrators of the Elector. Here they were important agents of the spread of reform, either by allowing evangelical preachers on their own estates, or by permitting a free dissemination in the countryside, reporting to the Elector, and carrying out his policy of favouring reform where it presented no threat of social or political unrest.

We could sum up the main sociological features of the reform movement as follows. The movement began in the towns, led by disaffected members of the established clergy, and it found its most enthusiastic response from the urban classes, who were undoubtedly attracted to it in considerable, if variable, numbers. It became a genuinely mass movement by finding support in the countryside, perhaps because of the undeniably social aspects of its message. Following the defeat of the peasants' revolt, the rural movement quickly lost its impetus, and perhaps the real numerical strength of its enthusiastic support thereafter was left to the towns.

Social elites played a vital role in the movement's development, providing political expertise and protection. It was initially a spontaneous movement, but without the backing of governing elites, from urban magistrates to territorial officials and princes, it would probably have lacked the political skill to survive. By the same token, it may well have developed more successfully as a social–evangelical movement, creating radical social and political change (see Chapter 5). After a brief period of mass enthusiasm, it retreated to being a minority phenomenon. At a crude estimate, during the first generation of the Reformation, up to mid-century, and perhaps even during the second, probably no more than 10 per cent of the German population ever showed an active and lasting enthusiasm for reformed ideas. Where massive numbers were 'won' after 1526 to what became the new church, it occurred involuntarily, through a prince deciding that his territory should adopt the new faith. When we speak of the extensive hold 'Protestantism' had on Germany by the second half of the sixteenth century (Ranke once estimated that 80 per cent of the population was Protestant at this time), this was because there were large numbers of 'involuntary Protestants' created by the princes' confessional choices. If 'the Reformation' became successful, it was something rather different from the wave of evangelical enthusiasm that swept through Germany in the early 1520s.

5 Politics and the Reformation

From the very beginning, the question of religious reform was so inextricably linked to political issues that it could never give rise to an unpolitical Reformation. Politics created complications at three levels, most of which overlapped: ecclesiastical, communal, and territorial-imperial politics.

(i) Ecclesiastical politics

It is important to recall that the church of that age was a *proprietary church*. That is, it rested on a structure of benefices with patrons both lay and ecclesiastical, who regarded church positions as their property and whose claims were upheld by the law. Any attempt at reform which involved changing the purposes of endowments, or changing incumbents against the will of patrons, was likely to involve lengthy negotiations, and could incur expensive and protracted lawsuits. It could also provoke political measures by the injured parties. The control of the nobility over the higher offices of the German church was so great that it has been labelled a 'nobles' church (*Adelskirche*), and they were not slow to take political reprisals where they felt their privileges had been infringed. Where control was exercised by powerful ecclesiastical corporations, such as monasteries, chapters or religious orders, they too were influential enough to call on the aid of other political powers.

As soon as popular movements began to demand appointment of preachers, cessation of masses and the funding of a preaching ministry such problems emerged. Unless money could be found to appoint to a wholly new position, an evangelical preacher could be obtained only by taking over an existing benefice. If the patron would not accept the new appointment or agree to waive his rights, there was no choice but to defy him and await the consequences. If necessary, the protection of some secular authority would have to be sought, who could guarantee assistance against reprisals. These considerations favoured easier reform in towns where there were already funded preacherships, where city magistrates controlled appointments, or where parishes elected their own pastor. Thus, in most towns the initial stages of reform depended at the very least on the goodwill and protection of the town council. And where the town council was not itself a sovereign body (as it often claimed to be in imperial cities), it was also dependent on the acquiescence of the territorial lord. The first example of formal, institutional ecclesiastical reform was that begun in Wittenberg in 1521–22, but all steps of reform had to secure the approval of the Elector of Saxony. Similarly, in Zwickau, the Saxon town which quickly followed Wittenberg with an institutional reform, the town council directed reform of the church, but it kept the Elector of Saxony carefully informed at each step, and virtually acted as an executor of the sovereign prince.

From the very beginning, then, *the institutionalisation of reform was an erastian phenomenon*: that is, the church was subjected to the control of secular authority. The traditional Lutheran view of this has been to fall back on Luther's doctrine of the two kingdoms, which emphasised the complete separation of the spiritual from the secular realm, allowing a civil ruler only a limited protective power over the church and the right to regulate 'externals'. Oberman has recently suggested that this was a doctrine formulated on the spur of the moment to meet a special set of circumstances. The devoutly Catholic ruler of the Duchy of Saxony, Duke George the Bearded, was effectively resisting reform in his territories, which often interpenetrated the lands of the Electorate of Saxony. Luther's 'new' doctrine (it was, in fact, simply a revised form of the medieval doctrine of the 'two swords') justified a refusal to recognise his competence in religious matters. However, Luther was perfectly willing to encourage a ruler to impose reform on his subjects when it would lead to his introducing 'right belief'. Thus, in 1525 he advised the Grand Master of the Teutonic Knights to secularise his territories, declare himself a secular prince, and introduce religious reform, by which means many souls would be 'won for the Gospel'.

Luther's distinctions proved to be difficult to maintain in practice, especially the ruler's control over 'externals' (debate over this contentious area was to divide Lutheranism for several generations!). In electoral Saxony the 'two kingdoms' distinction had little real practical meaning. By 1527–28 the erastian position was confirmed by the first Saxon Church Visitation, carried through by virtue of the Elector of Saxony's secular power as a 'Christian prince' (74). The various acts of legislation establishing the formal framework of church reform throughout Germany and Switzerland also attest the effective control of the church by the secular power. Almost everywhere this was achieved by means of Ecclesiastical Statutes (*Kirchenordnungen*), issued by secular authorities to regulate religion, in much the same way as other 'policing' legislation regulated many other areas of life. The institution of ecclesiastical reform was the conclusion of a long struggle between church and state over who should control ecclesiastical life, and the state clearly emerged as the victor. This trend was inherent in the evangelical movement from its very beginning, although its clerical leaders were scarcely aware of its implications. Perhaps they were too preoccupied with the second kind of political struggle which became caught up in the development of the movement.

(ii) Communal politics

From the fourteenth through to the sixteenth century we can point to a long-running political struggle in both town and country to defend communal forms of government. At issue were the rights of self-government of urban and rural communities. These were based on a notion of the contractual nature of power, in contrast to a hierarchical view which asserted that power was devolved from above (132). This latter view held that sovereign authorities were responsible

37

for their power to God alone, although they might delegate it to others beneath them.

In the towns this struggle was fought around the issues of communal rights and the rights of equal citizens: freedom of speech and assembly, freedom from arbitrary arrest, free access to political office, and the responsibility of government to the citizens, symbolically expressed in the annual accounting made to the commune. These issues were often embodied in the slogan of *gemein nutz versus eigen nutz*, the 'common weal' as opposed to individual self-interest. The 'common weal' involved a consensus among free citizens to preserve collective peace and order, to promote the common good of all, and to reconcile sectional interests. The principle of the 'common weal' was the dominant ideology in most towns with communal constitutions, and even their ruling elites paid lip-service to it. But at the end of the fifteenth century there was an unmistakable trend towards oligarchical government, whereby town governments regarded themselves not as representatives elected by equal citizens, but as sovereign bodies ruling over subjects and responsible to no one beneath them (72, 76, 81).

The communal mentality found an affinity with a number of ideas in the evangelical message. The basic premise of the communal movement was echoed in the idea of the equality of all Christians. The doctrine expressed by Luther in 1522, that a Christian congregation had the power to appoint and dismiss its own pastor, was but the corollary in church life of the communal principle in secular government. The notion that the activity of the individual inspired by faith and Christian love should be directed to the good of one's neighbour was but a religious version of the idea of the 'common weal' (65, 137).

Anticlericalism was another sensitive point in the communal outlook which the evangelical message was able to touch successfully. The privileges and exemptions of the clergy provide perhaps the greatest of urban grievances, since the clergy had always resisted incorporation into civic society on the grounds of their special status as servants of God. The doctrine of the priesthood of all believers provided a powerful theological justification for abolishing this privileged

38

status, and subjecting them to civic responsibilities such as taxes, excise and watch duty. This was further strengthened by the notion that the ordinary lay person could interpret the source of Christian truth as easily as the cleric. Anticlericalism was so strong in the towns that many town councils, led by shrewd politicians, were able to direct popular anger against the clergy, and so avert attention from wider social and economic issues (66).

The evangelical message brought a greater breakthrough for the peasantry. The same struggle for communal autonomy can be traced in the countryside, with the peasantry seeking self-government in autonomous village communes over several generations of resistance and rebellion before 1520 (36, 85). The evangelical message brought to this long tradition of peasant protest the sanction of a higher authority for their demands and grievances, the Word of God, a more concrete form of the 'divine law' to which they had sometimes appealed earlier. The Word of God as they understood it taught that serfdom was contrary to the freedom of Christians, that tithe was not justified in the Bible, and that any demands not founded on the Word of God should be held to be invalid (36, 82).

Peter Blickle has seen the communal principle as so important for the reform movement that he speaks of a 'communal Reformation' (*Gemeindereformation*) (11). The combination of evangelical ideas and communal principles was powerful enough to link together the differing interests of town and country into a potential revolution. The insistence on creating a true Christian community, based on principles of social justice founded in the Bible, was sufficiently subversive of a hierarchical feudal society to threaten its overthrow. As the Peasants' War gathered momentum in 1524–25, it seemed as though this revolution would indeed occur. The Twelve Articles, the main manifesto of the rebellious peasants, gave an ideological lead, and began to create an ideological unity over and above local allegiances (36, 46, 82). There are certainly problems about how far the Articles represented the views of the peasants, rather than the ideals of a few educated leaders (61), and the principles of the communal movement contained certain utopian features which would have been difficult to work out in practice. However, there is no doubt that they would have led to a radical restructuring of the society if implemented. This is shown in the most detailed expression of these ideas in the statutes drafted for the Tyrol by the revolutionary peasant leader Michael Gaismair (82).

There has been much debate on how far this upheaval of 1524–26 represented an attempt at an 'early bourgeois revolution'. The concept has many weaknesses, given the leading role of the peasantry and the unreliability of the towns during the Peasants' War, but many of the main ideas and leaders did come from the milieu of the urban middle classes. There seems to be no doubt that the socio-economic pressures of a developing early capitalism and of an agrarian feudalism attempting to revive itself after a period of crisis in the fifteenth century played a part in generating discontent and provoking the rebellion. Until we have more studies of social and economic developments, it is too soon to pronounce on the concept of an 'early bourgeois' movement, but the concept of a 'communal Reformation' has brought the question back to the centre of discussion after historians hostile to any notion of socio-economic causation influencing the Reformation had long tried to ignore it (see 5, 8, 9).

The fate of the evangelical-social movements, with their idealistic proposals for radical social and religious reform, was largely sealed with the defeat of the Peasants' War. Both lay and clerical leaders of the evangelical movement tried even more ardently than some of them had before 1524 to detach religious reform from social protest. The rights of secular authorities were upheld by reformed preachers. Those preachers who were only mildly critical of secular authority, much less those with genuinely radical ideas, were quickly silenced or removed from their posts. The mayor of Zwickau, Hermann Mühlpfort, himself a determined opponent of disturbance, complained in 1525 that henceforth people would have to keep quiet on matters of injustice, or else risk being called rebellious (44).

Yet the end of the peasants' revolt did not put an end to communal movements, nor to the phenomenon of religious reform linked to socially radical demands. There were towns in north Germany where religious reform appeared after 1526 virtually as social revolution, especially in Lübeck in 1528–30 and in Hannover in 1533–34. But the number and frequency of these incidents was nothing comparable to those of the years 1520–26, nor was there any similar sympathy of town and country. Indeed, although there was continuing rural unrest, rural evangelical-social movements seem to die out, until their reappearance in Austria at the end of the sixteenth century (see 142: *ch 8*). In this sense, reform as a broad popular movement was certainly finished by 1526. The final fate of reform fell even more decisively into the hands of sovereign authorities, who reasserted hierarchical principles, even when this was sometimes disguised in communal forms.

There was one variant of the 'communal Reformation' which did survive beyond 1526, the phenomenon called 'civic righteousness' (54, 65). 'Civic righteousness' took up and developed the medieval notion that the religious and secular fates of an urban community were inextricably linked, and it embodied four central ideas:

(1) The perfection of the individual Christian occurs in socio-political as well as in religious life.
(2) There are no religiously neutral areas of life – all forms of human activity are involved in one's salvation.
(3) The role of civil government is to strive to produce this perfection, or at least the optimal conditions for it, under the guidance of 'God's Word'.
(4) This places a heavy responsibility on civil magistrates to rule in a godly manner, as it does on the minister of God's Word to direct this activity.

The notion of civic righteousness was very much the product of an urban community which saw itself as Christendom in miniature (65). It was an emphasis found in Zwingli's view of the church in Zurich and Martin Bucer's in Strasbourg. In theory, it allowed a greater political role for the church than was conceded in other forms of Christian polity that were to emerge during the sixteenth century (54, 58, 79, 80). In practice, however, the role of the church was pushed into

41

subordination to the secular interests of the state, and although it was cherished as an ideal in many south German imperial cities the principle of 'civic righteousness' was to be realised only in Calvin's Geneva. Here, with the aid of the Consistory and a strict discipline over all aspects of civic life, Calvin strove to create a bibliocracy, rule by God's Word as found in the Bible and interpreted by its ministers (78). As a principle worked out in a small-scale urban society, it could not withstand the transition to a larger social setting, such as a principality or a kingdom. Martin Bucer attempted to map such a transition, with his advice to the young king Edward VI of England, *On the Kingdom of Christ*, but no attempt was ever made to put this blueprint into action.

(iii) Territorial-imperial politics

It has not been sufficiently realised how far the introduction of institutionalised reform was dictated by territorial and imperial politics. Few towns or territories could take a decision for reform without balancing the external alongside the internal political consequences. Towns, in particular, had to consider the danger to their economies from political reprisals by hostile princes or by the Emperor (137). Reutlingen was cited before the Imperial Government in 1525 (the only imperial city to be so cited), and was lucky to escape, largely because of the inactivity of the opponents of reform and the growing threat of the peasants' revolt (130). Even imperial cities were constrained by fears of such actions, some putting off reform, as did Esslingen, rather than risk imperial displeasure. They had to walk a political tightrope, hoping that the patience of their evangelical citizens would not be stretched to breaking point while they waited for the opportune moment. Some towns waited for a generation, as did Speyer and Regensburg (67). Others such as Augsburg sought the moment when they believed they were least likely to suffer from outside interference (56, 57). Many used the occasion of the Peasants' War to create a *fait accompli*, which they could claim had been forced upon them by their 'rebellious' citizens (66). Some were faced with such powerful clerical interests within their own walls that they held back almost completely from reform. This occurred most often in episcopal cities; even when the bishop no longer resided in some of these towns, they still contained powerful chapters (68). Some towns attempted to build on traditional allegiances with other towns, in order to provide mutual aid in the introduction and dissemination of reform (130). This pattern was noticeable in north Germany, among the Hansa towns, although the pattern of external pressure there was not sufficiently distinctive to create a 'Hansa town Reformation', as has recently been argued (83).

On the imperial stage, all towns found themselves subject to stronger powers than themselves. Ultimately, it was the ability of princes to adopt the new ideas and to implement them in their territories that turned reform into 'Reformation', providing sufficient institutional basis for us to speak meaningfully of a new church. The 1526 Recess of the Diet of Speyer was decisive. It allowed the estates to proceed in the matter of religion as the Word of God and the laws of the empire required. Since the 'evangelical' estates did not recognise the Edict of Worms as binding, they took this formulation as permission to move ahead with structured reform. Some towns took advantage of the Recess, but it was most useful to princes, such as those of Saxony and Hesse. This gave a constitutional ground for reform, which grew into a 'right of reformation'. The imperial attempts in 1529 and 1530 to reassert the Edict of Worms led to constitutional crisis, with the 'evangelical' estates falling back on a long-established politico-legal practice of *protestatio*. The idea of a legal and constitutional 'right of reformation' was finally conceded in 1555, and benefited the princes more than any other estate. The cities were not, of course, entirely helpless, and tried to pursue their own 'evangelical politics'. However the restoration of Duke Ulrich of Wurttemberg in 1534 (he had been expelled in 1519, and his territory occupied by the Habsburgs) meant that the dominant power in south-west Germany was now an erastian Protestant prince, long hostile to urban liberties. Ironically, he had been restored with the help of Strasbourg! (73).

There were examples of spontaneous urban reform in the second half of the sixteenth century, especially in the 'late city Reformation', but reform was never able to extricate itself from the embrace of the princes, and its fate became bound up with theirs (137). Their 'right of reformation' involved the creation of large numbers of 'involuntary Protestants'. The one powerful exception to this trend, the Genevan variant of reform, itself faced the same difficulties when it tried to expand outside the Swiss city republics.

6 Varieties of Reformation

One of the least edifying features of the reform movement was the way in which many of its participants were stigmatised and condemned by their fellow 'evangelical Christians'. From the end of the 1520s, an emergent 'Protestant' orthodoxy consistently denigrated many who held evangelical ideas with which they did not agree, labelling them as 'fanatics' (*Schwärmer*), as obstinate and malicious deviants who fomented unrest and disturbance (92). Modern historiography discusses these stigmatised groups under the heading of Anabaptists or Radicals, and although they are now accorded more attention than they were in the past (96, 101–3), they are still seen as somehow marginal to the development of the 'mainstream' Reformation. This is a measure of how far the confessional historiography produced by erastian churches has influenced views of the Reformation, obscuring the fact that there were many strands in the original evangelical movements. These strands will not be discussed here using the labels created by confessional historiography. It will be more fruitful to single out the issues on which the various tendencies began to diverge, in order to understand how different groups of reformers began to separate themselves from one another.

The first question to divide the reformers was the extent and speed of reform. This became clear even as the first ecclesiastical reforms were being implemented in Wittenberg in 1521–22. These found a wide measure of agreement among the Wittenberg reformers, although the real driving force was Andreas Bodenstein von Karlstadt. Karlstadt wanted radical measures: the abolition of the Mass, the giving of communion under both kinds, the abolition of a distinct priesthood and the allowance of clerical marriage.

He carried others with him, especially Luther's disciple Philip Melanchthon, not surprisingly since the reforms implemented ideas not dissimilar from Luther's own. However, Luther opposed the reforms. First, he believed they were causing disturbance by moving too fast, and so causing scandal to those with 'weak consciences'. (By this Luther meant those who either did not agree with the reforms, or did not understand why they should be implemented.) Second, Karlstadt wished to push ahead with reform without waiting for approval from secular authority (88, 93–5). Both issues were to continue to plague Lutheran attempts at reform, especially the first, and in the second half of the sixteenth century Lutheranism found itself criticised by the Calvinists for having made compromises with the old religion and for not having carried reform far enough.

The matter of secular approval of reform was also a continuing problem. For Luther, the ideal solution was a situation where secular authority assumed a benevolent neutrality, and allowed reform to proceed through clerical leaders, whose efforts the authorities would later recognise and institutionalise. Where the secular authority was openly hostile, as with Duke George of Saxony, Luther found himself in a dilemma. He could scarcely advise acting against a secular ruler, and in this situation he developed the doctrine of the two kingdoms. This separated the spiritual from the secular realm, and allowed him to argue that such an ungodly ruler had no authority over the individual conscience. But the individual believer could not oppose him directly, only witness his or her faith and endure the consequences (75).

Luther here diverged considerably from other reformers, who believed that political action was necessary to further reform. Zwingli took this stance in Zurich, although he tempered it with the view that one should as far as possible work through established secular authority. He parted company with many of his fellow evangelical Christians in Zurich analogous to Luther's falling out with Karlstadt. Zwingli wished reform to move in two stages: the city council should be convinced of the necessity of religious reform, and then, acting as the secular authority, it should see to its implementation. He thus favoured a process of continual pressure on the council to accede to reform, and he took any favourable reaction from its side as a signal to apply further pressure, until it had moved to the right position to sponsor change (103). This kind of dialectic characterised the process of reform in many Swiss and German towns. In practice, Luther's position was probably not very different from that of Zwingli, since both reformers envisaged a reform under different degrees of secular tutelage (130). The alternative position was that reform should be forced 'from below', if not exactly through popular pressure, certainly through the pressure of the fervent, those who 'stood by the Word of God'. Some of Zwingli's adherents in the Zurich countryside were impatient of waiting for any kind of official approval and turned to direct action, so that the reform there took the form of a revolt against secular authority (103).

If Karlstadt and the Zurich 'radicals' represented this second position, the person who carried it to its strongest conclusion was Thomas Müntzer, the revolutionary reformer active in central Germany. Müntzer was driven by a radical apocalyptic vision, believing that the end of the world was imminent, and that the rule of God's elect, the Saints, would usher it in. In Müntzer's vision, this would rectify many of the glaring injustices suffered by Christians in the world. Initially he demanded with prophetic fervour that the princes should step in to further reform, to hasten the rule of the Saints. Here he was doing no more, although with more prophetic passion, than Luther had done in his 1520 *Address to the Christian Nobility*. However, Müntzer quickly went a step further, threatening the princes that if they did not fulfil their Christian duty, they would suffer the wrath of God, and that the task of rooting out the ungodly would be taken up by the Saints themselves (95–6, 99).

We could characterise from these examples four attitudes on the speed and extent of reform:

(1) Luther: waiting for the believer and tarrying for the magistrate.
(2) Karlstadt: tarrying neither for the believer nor for the magistrate.

47

(3) Zwingli: political pressure on the magistrate to further reform.

(4) Müntzer: reform by violent action, if necessary against the magistrate.

The call to violent direct action for reform (note: action not by the masses, but by the elect of God) seemed to find an echo in the Peasants' War, especially in Müntzer's role in its Thuringian phase.

But Müntzer was not the only reformer to advocate an active millennarianism. The same view was found in others who had been involved in and survived the peasants' revolt: Hans Römer and Hans Hut. Römer was a furrier active around Erfurt, who preached that the Last Days would come in 1528, and who plotted to seize Erfurt at the end of 1527 in order to establish the New Jerusalem there. Hans Hut also expected the End in 1528, but recommended staying the sword over the ungodly until it appeared (97, 101). Melchior Hoffman also favoured millennarianism, but of a more passive kind. He expected the New Jerusalem to appear in Strasbourg, although he also did not advocate violent action to hasten its coming (100). However, there were other attempts to do so by seizing other towns, especially in the Netherlands; but it was not until the seizure of Münster in Westphalia that the idea of the New Jerusalem and the rule of the Saints was put into full practice.

The lurid history of Münster, written largely by those who opposed it, was used to stigmatise any radical variant of reform, and this has obscured some of the continuity between the Münster rebels and the 'mainstream' reform movement. This continuity can be found in three points. First, all reformers shared their belief that the End was imminent, Luther the foremost among them. Luther did not believe that the date could be so precisely determined, or that the End could be hastened by human activity, but a strong current of apocalyptic belief continued to colour his attitude towards the papacy and Catholicism (89), and apocalyptic fervour became a constituent element of later sixteenth-century Lutheranism, which cannot be understood if it is ignored. Second, the idea of a 'holy city' from which reform would

48

emanate was also strong among other reformers, and many saw Wittenberg in that role. However, it never achieved the same status as a charismatic centre as Mount Tabor did for the Bohemians. Something comparable was first found in a sober, non-millennarian form in the role ascribed to Geneva in the second half of the century. Third, the use of political action, if necessary with force, to push through reform against the will of 'ungodly' secular authority was not confined to radicals. It was to be taken up again by the next generation of reform inspired by Calvin.

Another issue which was to divide the reformers concerned the Word and the ministry of the Word. This was also posed at the very outset, by the appearance in Wittenberg of the Zwickau prophets, men who claimed to have had a personal revelation, and to interpret the Word of God under the inspiration of the Holy Spirit. Subsequent Lutheran accounts have depicted them as outrageously subjective, although their distance from Luther may not be all that great; certainly Melanchthon believed so at the time. Luther's insight into the nature of Pauline justification was, after all, a highly subjective matter, almost a personal revelation. It was also common from the early 1520s until well into the eighteenth century to depict Luther as speaking under the special inspiration of the Holy Spirit. The Zwickau prophets did not raise the problem of subjective, personal inspiration so much as the acute question of who was able authoritatively to interpret the Word of God.

It was a common theme in the popular literature of the reform movement that the 'common man' could read and understand the Bible as authentically as the clergy. Indeed, the 'common man' was presented as better able to preach the Word (although in practice few 'common folk' did turn to preaching). As this view spread, it brought with it the fear that students would abandon learning as useless, that lecture halls would stand empty and scholarship would be despised. Many universities did experience a dramatic drop in their numbers in the years 1520–22. In 1523 the Erfurt humanist Eobanus Hessus wrote to Wittenberg complaining about this trend, requesting testimonials from Luther and Melanchthon supporting the value of university study.

Both spoke out positively in favour of humanist (linguistic) studies for understanding Scripture and in 1524, perhaps influenced by Hessus' complaint, Luther addressed a tract to secular authorities, exhorting them to maintain schools. He argued that humanistic linguistic studies were a necessity, for without knowledge of the Biblical languages no one could rightly expound Scripture or decide on doctrine (17). As this decision was put into practice by the emergent state churches, it denied lay folk the right to read and interpret the Bible for themselves. Indeed, the conflict over infant baptism, which was to separate Luther from the Anabaptists, was largely a dispute over who could read the Bible aright, for the Anabaptists claimed (correctly, and to the great chagrin of their opponents!) that infant baptism could nowhere be deduced from the Bible (92). It also introduced an element of differentiation between laity and clergy as great as that which had separated them under the old church. The clergy were to be trained in Latin and Greek, so allowing them to participate in a 'learned culture', as opposed to the 'lay culture' of those who spoke and understood only German (105, 123).

Associated with this point of division, so rapidly achieved, was another over the rights of communities to elect their own pastors. As we have seen, Luther's argument of 1522 that Christian communities had the right to elect or dismiss their own pastors, and that secular authorities ought to acquiesce in that choice, found a strong response in both town and country. But by 1524 he had begun to retreat from that principle, decisively influenced by a confrontation with Karlstadt, who was now preaching in Orlamünde. Luther accused his enemy of preaching there without a proper call, but when Karlstadt was supported both by the community and the town council as having been elected and approved by them, Luther turned to higher authority. He now qualified the right of a congregation to elect its own pastor by insisting on the need for approval of secular authority. Given that Karlstadt's appointment was already approved by the immediate secular authority, the town council, Luther was actually appealing above it to princely authority. He proceeded to smear the Orlamünde congregation as a 'mob', arguing that they 'did not have the right to elect a pastor ... because that was the affair of the prince and his laws'! They should not 'interfere with the rights, property and authority of the territorial ruler' (88, 90).

We have discussed in a previous chapter the idea of a communal Reformation. With these two steps, this ideal was rejected by the Lutheran variant of reform in favour of a hierarchical church. It was to be hierarchical in two ways. First, through the establishment of a clerical church, eventually with an episcopate in all but name. Indeed, we can agree with those 'radicals' who argued that Lutheranism gave rise to a neo-clericalism which removed the congregational rights envisaged in the first stages of reform (53). Second, the church was to be subject to territorial princely authority. Even if the election of pastors did remain in some places, it had little real meaning if the final decision was taken by the secular authority. It is no surprise that in 1525 Luther should have commented negatively on the first of the Twelve Articles, which demanded that each parish be allowed to elect its own pastor. Luther insisted that a congregation which desired a minister 'should humbly ask the authorities for him'. If the request were refused, they could elect and support him at their own cost, but if the authorities still refused to accept him, there was no other option than that he should flee elsewhere, and his congregation with him (90).

It has been pointed out that one of the great divisions in the reform movement arose around this congregational principle, and the desire to actualise in practice the priesthood of all believers. Those groups stigmatised as Anabaptists were primarily groups moved by anticlericalism to oppose a hierarchical church, and to assert a genuinely congregational form of organisation. In as far as the reform movement can be said to be largely a 'communal Reformation', they represented its authentic ideals far more than the state-backed Lutheran churches that were quickly established on the basis of Luther's position.

But the rifts within the reform movement did not stop there. Everyone is familiar with the dispute between Luther and Zwingli over the Eucharist (7), but there were continuing

51

wrangles within Lutheranism itself over 'sacramentarian' doctrine which extended into the 1560s and 1570s. Indeed, Lutherans were split on many issues. As early as the 1530s, there were disputes about whether an unordained minister could preach, which went on into the 1550s. Luther quickly fell out with other 'Lutherans' over his own doctrines. From 1536 he was involved in a dispute with Johann Agricola's assertion that the Gospel freed people from the Law. Agricola was accused of being an antinomian and of encouraging libertinism. He was imprisoned in 1539, but was able to flee to Berlin. In 1553 George Major, Superintendent (Bishop) of Eisleben, and former Professor of Theology in Wittenberg, was accused of error for arguing the value of good works (though he did not claim they assisted salvation). Justus Menius, one of the earliest enthusiasts for Luther's ideas in Erfurt, and subsequently the reformer of Gotha, was accused of apostasy because he seemed to be supporting Major – he had not condemned him strongly enough. In 1555 Menius thought it safer to put himself beyond the reach of his Lutheran ruler, and he fled from his post.

The most savage divisions within Lutheranism, however, arose after Luther's death, with disputes over the sanctity and inviolability of his teachings. Those who wished to regard all that Luther had written as 'sacred doctrine' as unalterable as Scripture itself were opposed by those who believed that Luther had not said the last word, and that reformed doctrine could be developed further. This led to the sorry sight of rival editions of Luther's works, from Jena and Wittenberg, each claiming to be the true heritage of the great man, like pre-Reformation clerics squabbling over the relics of a medieval saint. As early as 1559 there was an attempt to create an orthodoxy of 'right belief' in the Saxon Book of Confutation, which enumerated all those who deviated from its tenets: Anabaptists, sacramentarians, antinomians, adiaphorists (those who held that some ceremonies were a matter of free choice) and synergists (those who believed that people were not purely passive in their salvation by faith). These were not just academic disputes conducted in latinate theological tracts or in lecture rooms. They threatened life and limb in the same way that Catholicism threatened those it hereticated. We have mentioned the cases of Agricola and Menius, and they were not isolated instances. In 1559 two leaders of the synergists were hauled from their beds at night by a troop of armed men, and left to contemplate the consequences of false doctrine in prison. In the early 1560s there were purges of the university of Jena, and thirty pastors were sent into exile for false belief (91).

It is no surprise that when Calvinism began to make progress in Germany, it did so largely at the expense of Lutheranism: everywhere it was formally introduced, it was in place of a Lutheran church. By 1568 Catholic polemicists could depict evangelical belief as dismembering itself, through a lurid broadsheet showing Luther's corpse being sliced up by squabbling followers. The 1580 Formula of Concord was an attempt to patch up these differences within Lutheranism, but not all Lutherans accepted it, and evangelical divisions continued into the seventeenth century and beyond. Clearly, the idea of a cohesive, uniform and normatively Lutheran Reformation is belied by these facts, yet the divergences within what became 'the Lutheran church' are usually ignored or underplayed in Reformation textbooks. If we look back to the 'original evangelical message', it was a long way from what had, by the end of the sixteenth century, become 'Protestantism'.

7 The Impact of Reform

Historians have often made very sweeping claims about the impact of the Reformation on religion, society and the state. These range from practical matters such as the reshaping of marriage laws, or the emergence of new forms of poor relief, to broad political developments such as the growth of the absolutist state, and vast generalisations about the emergence of capitalism or the development of 'secularisation' or 'modernisation'. Some of these latter claims display *par excellence* the teleological view of history, and bristle with so many question-begging prejudgments that they cannot be adequately discussed in so brief a space as is available here. It does seem certain, however, that recent research is leading us to such a different understanding of the Reformation, that many of these common notions about its impact should be drastically revised.

The most obvious area of impact was in the conduct and organisation of church life. Many traditional religious ceremonies and customs were abolished, as well as many traditional feast days. The most important, because of the impressive religious and secular ceremony with which it had been observed, was the feast of Corpus Christi, celebrating the Real Presence of Christ in the consecrated bread and wine. Religious worship was radically reshaped: the Mass became the celebration of the Lord's Supper, conducted in the vernacular by a minister in a plain black gown who faced the congregation over a table, using bread instead of a wafer, and who offered the cup to the laity. The sermon became more central to religious worship, and in some places a daily sermon replaced daily Mass, while the Lord's Supper was received infrequently, often no more than monthly, and sometimes only at Christmas and Easter. The only other

Sacrament recognised was Baptism, although Penance continued as a pious practice in some places. Marriage went through a curious change, for although it was no longer recognised as a Sacrament, the ceremony was made more religious than in the past, with a service in church being given greater prominence over secular celebrations (116).

These were significant changes, especially in the most radically reformed places, but there was wide variation in many Protestant communities. In some places the liturgy could appear much the same as it had under the old religion, and often the service book being used well into the later part of the sixteenth century was merely a German translation of the old Latin Mass Book. In parts of Saxony vestments and candles were used for the Lord's Supper, and until the middle of the century even the practice of the Elevation, holding aloft the consecrated bread for the adoration of the congregation. Many images were retained in Lutheran churches, while church buildings themselves saw only minimal alteration to adapt them to the new form of worship. It was not until 1618 that the first uniquely Protestant 'preaching church' was built, in Nidda in Hessen, resembling a meeting house more than a traditional church (133). In Brandenburg the liturgy retained much of its Catholic outward appearance, although it had turned Protestant in 1540. This was largely because of the affection of the Elector Joachim II for the colour and display of Catholic ritual, and many Catholic practices remained for the next sixty years (33).

The most marked changes were seen in the new clergy. They lost many of their old legal and financial privileges, removing one of the greatest causes of anticlericalism. Here, however, the reformers had merely supplied a theological justification for a trend already present during the fifteenth century, of subjecting the clergy to secular duties and responsibilities. More striking was the emergence of a married clergy, which brought them closer to married parishioners, and stabilised the lives of those unable to face the demands of celibacy (113). It also relieved lay fears about the sexual predatoriness of the old clergy: better to have married priests than have them chasing one's wife or daughters. Even so, the change was not as radical as has been claimed.

There was a centuries-old practice of *de facto* clerical marriage, by which numerous priests lived in stable long-term relationships with a common law wife and children. From the evidence of pre-Reformation visitation records, layfolk were less worried about this practice than the higher clergy, bishops anxious to enforce synodal statutes on celibacy. Nor did the introduction of a married clergy put an end to clerical sexual misdemeanours. Indeed, during the first generation of reform, as many former priests tried to sort out their relationships with their former concubines, it may even have increased them, with some pastors involved in bigamous or less than licit relationships. The greatest gainers from this reform were the clergy themselves, who could now enter marital relationships with a good conscience (47). It is difficult to avoid the conclusion that clerical marriage was largely a tidying up of a problem of the clergy, carried through by the clergy for the clergy.

Creating a reformed clergy did not remove the social gulf between them and the laity. We have already seen how ordination came to have much the same significance in the new churches as in the old, a mark of qualitative distinction between two orders. To this was added the creation of a trained graduate clergy, a continuation of the drive towards a professionalised clergy from the end of the fifteenth century. It was at first difficult to fill all positions with graduates, and many of the first generation of Lutheran pastors were former tradesmen, but by the end of the sixteenth century probably as many as 80–90 per cent of Protestant clergymen were university graduates (123). Gradually there grew up a clerical elite, whose sons became clergymen and married the daughters of clergymen, a clerical caste as distinct as the old.

This had the effect of accentuating the social distance between clergy and people. The pastor became a figure of social authority, with greater learning and social status than his parishioners. He was entrusted with the task of proclaiming right doctrine to a community which could no longer exercise the rights claimed by the early reform movement, of appointing or dismissing their own pastor, or determining right belief as a believing community. Instead the pastor was an arm of the state, enforcing moral and social order (63). The authoritarian trend was typified by the Saxon Church Ordinance of 1533, which prohibited anyone interrupting the pastor while he was in the pulpit or contradicting him in public.

We can assess the impact on broader lay life by looking at poor relief, marriage and the status of women, and education. In poor relief, the Reformation was not as innovative as has been claimed. Well before the advent of the evangelical movement, there was a clear trend towards the regulation of poverty and vagrancy, both as a means of regulating labour and of controlling civic expenditure. A distinction was introduced between the deserving local poor and the workshy, as well as between the local and the wandering poor. The wandering poor were not to be tolerated, and were to be forced to return to their place of origin. Gradually the attitude evolved that charity was a matter bounded by financial stringency, public hygiene, public security and social stability. This trend was general throughout western Europe, where begging was regulated or prohibited everywhere during the first half of the sixteenth century (111).

The new religious ideas provided theological justification for this trend in three ways. First, they removed the religious status of begging as a work pleasing to God (though there were also strong signs of this before 1520, in the view that the life of many vagrants was unchristian). Second, they stressed the Christian responsibility of the community to regulate poverty. Third, they removed the personal nexus in charity: giving alms became a purely impersonal act, usually in the form of a voluntary contribution to a Poor Chest. The Poor Chest was the sole institutional innovation of the reform movement, an idea suggested by Luther to the town of Leisnig in 1522, and subsequently followed by other Lutheran authorities. The proceeds from church properties and suspended religious foundations were to be placed in such a chest, thus creating a system of poor relief without any extra financial burden on the community. Nonetheless, many original donors objected to this procedure and sought to recover what they regarded as family property. This was a source of considerable tension with both religious leaders and civic authority. Indeed, in many Protestant areas, many individuals were reluctant to contribute to the upkeep of the poor by voluntary contributions, a sorry conclusion to the early evangelical ideal that a revived evangelical faith would move Christians to active expression of their love of neighbour.

In the realm of the family, sex and marriage, there were also significant changes. Lutheranism brought about a revaluation of sexuality and of the status of marriage. Sex was seen as a natural appetite, which was not sinful when satisfied within marriage, even when not strictly tied to the purpose of procreation. At the same time as they declared marriage to be no Sacrament, the reformers tried to raise its status as an ideal Christian estate, providing a superior context for service to God and one's fellow men through the family and the home. Patriarchy was the ideal held up for evangelical Christians in marriage and in the household, a hierarchical structure of obedience, in which a wife obeyed her husband, children obeyed their parents and servants their master. Here Lutheranism and other varieties of Reformation did little to shake the deep-seated sexual misogyny of the age, the fear of women as dangerous sexual beings who were best placed under the control of a husband and a household. (Perhaps only Anabaptism, with its strong emphasis on the fellowship of *all* Christians, male and female, managed to break out of this mould.) Because of the role accorded to parents in arranging the marriages of their children, the reformers also opposed clandestine marriages. Allied to this was a determined opposition to sex outside marriage. Thus, Protestant authorities acted to close down brothels, and prohibited popular mating customs which held that sex between 'betrothed' couples was not sinful (109, 113, 115, 143).

In surveying such developments, it is necessary to sift out what was original from what was not, to compare projected ideals with the reality, and to discern what was an ambivalent change with a two-edged effect. In their attitudes to clandestine marriages, the reformers were expressing nothing new, for both secular and ecclesiastical authorities had legislated against these before the Reformation, and had tried to insist on parental consent. Protestant authorities were no more successful than Catholic in preventing them, however, and they still gave rise to a good proportion of cases to come before marriage courts (118). Similarly, the attempt to outlaw pre-marital sex had mixed results. Public brothels were often closed, only to be replaced by unregulated prostitution, while Protestant authorities often operated a double standard by prosecuting prostitutes but not their male clients (115, 117). Cases continued to come before Protestant marriage courts no less than before Catholic from women who claimed that men had promised them marriage in order to sleep with them. Both types of court attempted to decide whether a valid agreement to marry was involved or merely fornication. The tendency in both kinds of court was to decide in the majority of cases in favour of the latter (118).

The Reformation's ambivalent impact can be seen in the case of the position of women in society. It is often said that Protestantism raised the status of women by projecting the ideal image of the Christian wife and mother. But it can also be said to have narrowed the range of acceptable female identities. The choice of an independent and celibate religious vocation in which a woman might develop her own talents was removed. In its place was set only the new ideal of the pastor's wife, to be fulfilled within the patriarchal context. Again, the rights of a woman to resist her husband's sexual demands were narrowed. Before the Reformation, sexual intercourse was prohibited at certain times of the year, and a woman could take advice from her confessor about what was or was not acceptable behaviour within marriage. Luther and other reformers, on the other hand, took the view that there were no unsuitable times, and that a wife had a Christian duty to fulfil her husband's demands, for otherwise he might fall into sin. Indeed, refusal of the conjugal debt constituted grounds for divorce (as it had under Catholicism). Divorce was certainly one area where reform brought some innovation, although Protestant authorities do not appear to have made it easy. They were concerned above all else to preserve stable domestic life (115, 118).

It has been said that Protestant marriage courts met the problems of lay people in the question of sex and marriage more effectively than their Catholic counterparts (118).

Yet Protestantism had no ideal outside of domestic bliss in the patriarchal family to offer single young people. At a time when late marriage was frequent among the peasantry and often an economic necessity for guild apprentices and journeymen, the young were seen only as an unruly element to be controlled – by pastor or parent (114). We also need to know more about the Reformation's real impact on popular practices, where the attempts at control by ecclesiastical and secular elites may actually have narrowed the options to lay people. 'Peasant marriages' were probably the most common form of rural union, stigmatised by Catholic and Protestant reformers as *wilde Ehen* – 'wild marriages', or common law marriages in modern terminology. Similarly, popular divorce was common, by simply moving away from an unpleasant spouse, or through formal leavetaking at a crossroads. By forcing such practices into marriage courts, Protestantism was simply continuing a pre-Reformation authoritarian trend.

We find in education another area where there seems to have been a decisive impact, although one whose effects have been questioned by recent research. One of the great ambitions of the reformers was to create pious Christians capable of reading the Bible and the Catechism. When Philip of Hesse introduced reform in his territories in 1536, his stated aim was to have a school in every town and village. Most reformed authorities shared this aim, introducing school ordinances regulating elementary education – by 1600 over 100 such had been introduced in Germany. Progress could be quite spectacular in the provision of schools: the Duchy of Wurttemberg had only 89 schools in 1520, but the number had grown to 150 by 1559 and to over 400 by 1600. Yet it is difficult to know how effective these schools were. In rural areas parents tended to keep their children home to help with agricultural work, and the problem was such that some states had to establish 'winter schools' to provide education in the agricultural off-season (108, 120, 122).

In theory such schools ought to have raised basic standards of literacy, and there is certainly evidence that they did so in some countries, such as Sweden. But recent studies warn against the assumption that more schooling meant higher literacy (108). Although we have very few extensive studies for Germany, Bernard Vogler's study of Zweibrücken to 1619 confirms the need for caution (122). In a pioneering study of Protestant education, backed by evidence from visitation records, Gerald Strauss has pointed to a failure of reformed education, suggesting that the new schools did not produce the pious educated Christians aspired to in the reformers' ideals. Indeed, visitations in rural parishes even two or three generations after the beginning of reform showed the people to be as ignorant of Christian belief as if the reform had never been (119–20). Strauss traced some of this failure to Protestant pedagogy, to stilted rote learning and a pessimistic attitude towards children which aimed at creating formal outward conformity without much attention to an inward state of piety (120, and see also 107). These findings have not been undisputed, although most criticisms so far have concentrated on challenging the validity of Strauss's sources and approach, rather than citing evidence to the contrary (106, 110). It has been shown that there was some marked advance in the parishes around Strasbourg in the late 1560s in educating the young as pious Protestants (110). But that we have to look so far afield, to forty years after the beginnings of the reform in Strasbourg, surely confirms Strauss's point: the slow and tentative nature of deep-rooted reception of reformed ideas (here see esp. 135).

Two other trends have been remarked which are relevant to Strauss's view. One was the attempt to 'reform popular culture', an attempt to eradicate many popular customs held to be of pagan origin or unchristian, or which were believed to undermine good morals or good order. Popular festivities such as Carnival fell particularly into this category, as did popular mating customs such as St John's Day festivities or May Day celebrations (20, 104). This was part of an attempt at 'christianisation', conducted by Protestant and Catholic reformers alike, and has been seen as the expression of a campaign to impose the culture of urban elites on an unruly countryside. The desire to discipline souls and bodies contributed to the development of a more ordered society, and in the view of one historian served the interests of the emerging absolutist state (121). Until more research has been done, it is difficult to confirm or deny such hypotheses. Certainly the clergy did become in many places agents of social control and arms of the civil bureaucracy, while the development of a learned ministry schooled in a Latin-reading humanist culture helped to confirm the division between 'learned culture' and 'lay culture', the latter restricted to use of the vernacular (105, 122).

A second trend, undoubtedly linked to the first, was a process of 'confessionalisation', the creation of a distinctively 'Protestant' cultural and social identity, with its own customs, behaviour and folklore, defined in part at least by hostility to the old religion. From its side, Catholicism assisted the process by Tridentine reforms specifically aimed at refuting Protestant doctrines and practices. The social and cultural nature of 'confessionalisation' still awaits investigation (a beginning has been made in the fine work by Hsia – see 140), although there are signs that it was not as rigid in practice as it attempted to be in theory. Mixed marriages were disapproved of by both confessions, but there is evidence that they occurred frequently. There were attempts to prohibit attendance at universities of rival confessions, but in the interests of scholarship, this boundary was frequently crossed. Nonetheless, an understanding of the nature and extent of confessionalisation is essential if we are to perceive how the fairly fluid reform movements of the sixteenth century developed into the rigid Protestantism of the seventeenth, which then attempted retrospectively to rewrite the history of reform to show itself as the only acceptable and natural outcome. This is a task which should occupy historians in the years ahead.

8 Supplementary Chapter

C. Scott Dixon

In the years since *The German Reformation* first appeared, many of the themes discussed in the text have found their way into the mainstream narratives of Reformation history. Scribner spoke of the need to imagine the Reformation as a 'complex, extended historical process, going well beyond the endeavours of one man or one tendency, and involving social, political and wider religious issues', and most modern studies of the German Reformation are guided by a similar spirit. The retreat from narrowly confessional religious history is largely complete, and it is now more or less commonplace for sociological and anthropological studies to appear in the same bibliographies as church histories and theological analyses. Schools of interpretation remain, but most scholars move between genres without giving it much thought, and most surveys of the period take in a broad range of ideas and approaches (**19, 46, 74, 95, 138**).

In the last few decades the historical landscape of the German Reformation has steadily changed: chronologies have shifted, events have multiplied, contexts have become more and more localised and complex, historical actors have grown in number, while the search for causes and consequences steadily revaluates the importance of the event. General histories are still possible, of course, but it is becoming difficult for one scholar to take all of the literature into account, and most recent syntheses have focussed on particular features of the national setting, such as the political framework or the cultural conditions in the German lands, rather than attempt to write comprehensive histories of the event (**16, 30, 113**). If the amount of literature is anything to

65

go by, Scribner's view that the German Reformation should be seen as 'involving social, political and wider religious issues' is certainly shared by scholars. In many ways, the problem is not the poverty of perspectives, but the growing wealth.

These days it is not unusual for scholars to speak of Reformations rather than a single Reformation in order to emphasise the protean nature of the movement. This is an accommodating perspective, for while it can preserve the traditional narrative of the Reformation as a religious event (and in particular Martin Luther's struggle with the Roman Catholic Church), it can also tolerate a range of other approaches, whether social, cultural, or political in inspiration. However, it can only do this by abandoning the long-held notion that *the Reformation* marks a fundamental turning point in European history, for in place of a singular event we now have parallel developments, and in place of an established place of origin, associated causes, and a fairly clear trajectory from beginning to end, we now have a number of contending narratives, each one historically unique and historically relevant.

How we speak of the event, in the singular or the plural, has fundamental implications for how we make sense of it. As a recent dialogue between Reformation historians made clear, different starting points can give rise to widely different conclusions (**51**). For those historians who stress the role played by individuals in history, the importance of Luther was paramount, for it was his religious insights and his personal actions that sparked and then propelled the movement. It is impossible to understand the event free of his influence. For other historians, it does not really make sense to speak of the force of personality or look for a central figure in the early Reformation, for it soon took on local colour once it left the confines of Wittenberg. In the shifting constellation of public personalities, no one voice dominated. Still other historians look for the essence of the event in ideas rather than individuals and thus imagine the history of the Reformation as an episode in the evolution of religious thought. There are continuities with the theology of the medieval period, but there are clear and fundamental points of division as well, and it is these vital ideas, and their associated social and cultural implications, that should sit at the heart of our understanding. A broad array of other approaches could be added to these three, but the point has been made. The difference between Reformation and Reformations entails more than just a turn of phrase. It runs deep.

(i) Reformation myths

One thing that seems to have remained fairly consistent in the study of the Reformation is the fascination scholars have with Martin Luther. Of course, as the established founder of the evangelical movement in Germany, it is only natural that he should attract so much attention. For this reason, and others besides, his personal history continues to be a theme of great interest, even if the complexity of his religious thought and the sheer fullness of his life make considerable demands on the biographer (**12–14, 76**). At the same time, however, we continue to move farther and farther away from the notion caricatured at the outset of this book, the idea that Luther should be portrayed as a 'great sage, a spiritual colossus' who took a heroic personal stand against the medieval Catholic Church and then single-handedly orchestrated the course of the Reformation. Recent studies of the rise of Luther's celebrity have begun to focus more on the public perception (and later fabrication) of his image than rely on the details of the traditional histories. For instance, in the years immediately following the posting of the theses, Luther was not primarily known to the general public as an outspoken theologian engaged in a war of words with the papacy. His early popularity was due to his appeal as the author of fairly traditional works of pastoral and devotional literature (**32, 81–2**). The image we have inherited of Luther as the relentless nemesis of the Roman Catholic Church is a later development. In part, the changing image was the product of evolving historical circumstance, but it was also fabrication, the projection of a general idea of Reformation that had little to do with historical reality.

Scholars have to keep this balance in view, for few historical figures have been the subject of so much symbolic manipulation over the years as Luther. Even in his own lifetime he was portrayed in different ways, from saint, prophet, and holy man, to scourge of the papacy and the champion of the German Nation (**70, 125**).

To a greater extent than many other important events in the past, the German Reformation forces the historian to come to terms with the relationship between the individual in history and the broader forces of change. The sixteenth century was a vital stage in the development of Europe, and there were already a number of profound developments in train before Luther proposed a reform of the church. At the same time, no previous period in European history was witness to so many individuals emerging onto the public stage with ideas and opinions of their own. What is the proper balance between these two dimensions of the movement? To what degree was the Reformation shaped by its inspirational leaders? It is an important question, especially as it is so easy to identify the movement with certain figures and then associate the historical details with the ideas or the actions of these people. Traditionally, the history of the German Reformation has corresponded closely to Luther's own vision of the movement, and that is one of the main reasons why he has been given such a prominent role. But there were many other reformers in the German lands, and many other visions of reform, and it may be a distortion to suggest that the best way to get in touch with the past is by way of the dominant perspective.

Thomas Müntzer, for example, had profound differences with the Wittenberg notion of reform, both with the theological principles and the social and political aspects, and yet because he has been associated with the radical fringe, and because this tradition was historically less successful than the Lutheran variety, the radical Reformation and its leaders have always been situated on the margins of the main event (**36, 117**). These days, historians have begun to look more closely at how certain reformers (along with the surrounding history) have been excluded or marginalised over the years in order to save the appearance of the traditional narrative. In the opinion of these scholars it is misguided to think of the German Reformation as a unitary phenomenon with a clear figurehead, an inner logic, and an obvious outcome. On the contrary, the Reformation was an intensively varied and contradictory conglomerate of leaders, interests and ideas, and it was not inevitable that the movement would take shape as it did (**40, 124, 140**).

Speaking of the Reformation as a 'complex, extended historical process' necessarily means reducing the role played by certain individuals and placing more emphasis on the impersonal forces of historical change. There is nothing new in this, of course, for historians have been associating the movement (or more strictly speaking the rise of Protestantism) with broader patterns of social, political and cultural change for centuries. The difficulty lies in identifying the relationship between the patterns already in evidence and the unique contribution of the Reformation. For instance, to what extent can the demands for religious reform be associated with the rise of sovereign communities in Germany? To what degree was evangelical theology a further expression of the changing intellectual habits of the age? Can this type of religious thought be captured in the themes of individualism, skepticism, or the primacy of personal judgement, so central to the European Renaissance? Or more generally, was the Reformation simply a prism for latent historical forces or was it a catalyst for fundamental change? Once associations between the Reformation and the vital context have been established, questions of this kind are unavoidable. Yet it can easily lead, as Scribner suggested, to a form of myth-making about the event and thus distort our understanding of the past. The best way to avoid this pitfall, as he says, is to try to guard against an overly teleological reading of history. This is not easy to do. It certainly helps to become more aware of how former narratives of the Reformation have been fashioned in the hope that this will fine-tune our senses to our own prejudices and points of view. One of the recent areas of interest has been Reformation historiography, the study of the way influential scholars have approached and interpreted the event, and it has contributed much to our sense of perspective (**23**).

But surely the most effective way is to get as close as possible to the views of the age, to listen to the voices of the people involved in the historical process and then determine which aspects of the vital context sit closest to the heart of concerns. For many Reformation historians, this means beginning with the study of religious culture.

(ii) Religion and reform

Scribner opened his discussion of religious culture in medieval Germany by taking stock of four interpretations of the age, each one fundamentally different from the others. That interpretations can range so widely is due to the scale of standards and values applied by historians. It is also partly due to the nature of the source materials. But the main reason for the variety of opinion lies in the basic assumptions underlying the analysis. For centuries historians have considered the Reformation to be one of the fundamental turning points in European history, the division between the medieval and the modern world (**31**). With this in mind, Reformation history has been cast in terms of contrasts – the old versus the new, the medieval versus the modern, the monolithic versus the plural. Recently, however, there has been a tendency to play down the idea of discontinuity. Most serious historians still hold that the Reformation was a profoundly important event, but at the same time they have started to move away from interpretations that project stark contrasts. Instead of portraying Reformation society as different in kind from the medieval world, interpretations now place more stress on the continuities and similarities of Catholic and Protestant developments (**97–8, 138**). Instead of fitting medieval religious culture into distinct analytical categories (popular versus elite, orthodox versus heretical, structure versus praxis), historians are now more sensitive to the different dimensions of religious life and emphasise how the faith developed as an ongoing dialogue between the institutional framework and the relative flux and flexibility of the liturgical experience (**135**). Instead of writing the intellectual history of the Reformation by contrasting the principles of Reformation theology with the corpus of Catholic thought, scholars have stressed the overarching continuities of the two traditions (**73**). Work of this nature represents an inclination rather than an innovation, for similar views have been aired before, but it is a significant historiographical turn nevertheless.

When studying the Reformation we should keep in mind that this was an age when people were becoming better informed and increasingly curious, not just about the natural world but the spiritual world as well. In religious matters, there was a growing tendency to emphasise certain aspects of the faith in an effort to cut through the surrounding complexity and get to the heart of the Christian message. There was a heightened need to understand, to order and to simplify, as the age sought 'the alignment of both religion and society towards a standardizing, authoritative, regulating and legitimizing focal point' (**49: 311**). It was not a revolutionary turn away from religion. On the contrary, the search for understanding drew many closer to the church.

Forms of religiosity varied. Among the elite, some believers withdrew from the world and spent hours in pious contemplation; some looked to Mary and the other advocates of mercy and sought salvation through intervention and mediation; others relied on the institutions of the Catholic church and encouraged a reform of the schools and the monasteries. While in the towns and villages, where the realities of life limited the possibilities, the parishioners made use of the religious means at their disposal, which often meant reliance on the sacramental objects of the local church or going beyond the bounds of traditional worship and joining guilds and brotherhoods. That is why there was so much sensuality in late-medieval worship, for it was rooted in the idea (derived from orthodox teaching) that the believer could attain knowledge of the divine by way of human endeavour. Indeed, the entire religious system was based on the assumption that there were points and moments of contact between the sacred and the profane. A prominent example of this way of thinking was the trust in the 'sacramental gaze', the widespread conviction that just by looking at a sacramental object such as the Eucharist the

71

believer would be infused with grace. But there were many other ways to establish personal contact with the divine, including the sacramental objects related to worship or the annual rites and festivals of the church – of which the *Corpus Christi* procession was perhaps the most impressive (**103**, **128**: **85–128**; **150**). In the years following the Reformation the Protestants would criticise these public displays of religious enthusiasm, but in truth they were symptomatic of the same need for assurance and understanding that set Luther on his spiritual path.

However we understand the background conditions, we must recognise that in its origins the Reformation was a religious event, which means that the causes and concerns at the heart of the conflict were rooted in the culture and teaching of the church. It began as a debate between clergymen – more specifically, between Luther and the defenders of traditional Catholicism. It had little to do with the broader concerns of public religious culture, and it only remotely touched on the theological themes that would later characterise the movement. In the beginning, it was essentially an issue of ecclesiastical authority. Luther had challenged the authority of the Catholic Church, its teachings on indulgences, its claims to supremacy and the sovereignty of its interpretation of scripture, and the papacy had responded by demanding immediate obedience and a return to the fold (**2**).

Even the most perceptive minds of the day viewed the origins of the conflict as an issue of authority. In the eyes of the Humanists (Erasmus being a notable exception), the essence of the affair was little more than a continuation of the debate between scholastic theologians and German Humanists over the valid interpretation of scripture. Again it was a question of authority, with Luther representing the views of the *studia humanitatis* and the papal theologians representing the views of scholasticism, and with the debate revolving around the secular themes associated with Humanism rather than the interpretation of canon law (**45**, **105**). But first impressions were deceiving. However it was initially perceived, the Luther affair did not remain a purely religious event for very long, and it soon became much more than just a quarrel between clergymen. Once the conflict had grabbed the attention of the public, and once the religious concerns started to fuse with the traditional grievances of the German Nation, the theological debate evolved into a revolutionary social and political movement. Understanding this process of transformation, both the inner logic and the external detail, is central to the interests of current historiography. The Reformation may have begun with the posting of the theses in Wittenberg, but as Luther himself later confessed, it soon took on a form and an energy that had very little in common with the original event.

(iii) The evangelical movement

With the rise of the evangelical movement, Luther's conflict with the Catholic Church became a national event. All manner of people began to take an interest in the religious debate and offer open support, from princes and city councillors to monks, peasants and artisans. Indeed, the sheer reach and energy of the movement has made it difficult to offer a satisfactory description of the early Reformation. Even the principles of evangelical theology, once a fairly stable point of reference, have become a matter of debate. In the traditional view, there was a clear and consistent message from the very outset. The fundamental insight was Luther's idea of justification (which remained the essential principle of Reformation thought throughout the century), but there were other ideas as well, including critical opinions of the Catholic Church, shared views on grace and salvation, new notions of the clerical estate, and the intense reliance on scripture in place of the traditional teaching of the church (**1, 55, 84**). Recently, however, the very notion of a broadly shared vision or coherent corpus of ideas has come into question. Some historians have argued that there was too much diversity and too many contending opinions to speak in any meaningful way of a unified intellectual agenda (**40, 61**). Even the notion of justification, it has been suggested, will not bridge the distance between the different Reformation movements in the German lands (**72**).

Without doubt, there was a broad canvas of opinion. One of the things that is most striking about the early Reformation literature, for instance, is the spectrum of people who wrote in support of Luther (or the associated cause) and the wide variety of views they held. Predictably, the disaffected clergy were the majority voice, but with the Reformation the laity also surfaced as a major force in the war of words and their sense of grievance gave rise to a completely new public dialogue. As any list of representative pamphlet titles would attest, in the early years notions of reform could range widely, from raw anticlericalism and impassioned nationalism to sophisticated programmes of secular and ecclesiastical change (**21**, **24**, **41**). The difficult task facing historians is to determine how the variety of opinion associated with the evangelical movement can find a point of origin in the Luther affair. In essence, it is less a question of identifying the formal principles of belief than following the translation of these principles into the religious language of the common man.

One of the fascinating things about the Reformation was the relationship that developed between the course of historical events and the perception of these events in the media. Historians have termed it the first media revolution of the modern age, and there is little doubt that it was the first time in history that so many views were made public through so many means (**16**, **32**, **52**). But it was not value-free reportage. In coming to terms with the use of the media during the Reformation, historians have grown more sensitive to the forms and traditions of communication that shaped the dialogue. The ideas in the early evangelical pamphlet literature, for instance, were as much a legacy of the medieval age as they were a fresh vision of the faith. There was already a tradition of religious grievance in place, as well as a language for its expression, and much of this reached the surface when the first supporters took up their pens in defence. A few spoke of justification through faith alone, but the majority referred to themes that had been in the public imagination for years before the posting of the theses, including the moral failings of the clerical estate and the corruption of the papacy (**21**, **39**, **134**).

Later in the century, as confessional tensions increased and the theological corpus grew in sophistication, the confessional discourse in the media became even more complex. Both Catholic and Protestant authors made full use of the skills imparted by a Humanist education to get their message across. The new genre of the pamphlet dialogue, though relatively simple in form, became a forum for sophisticated techniques of rhetoric and polemic. Indeed, the very fact that it was a new type of medium made it possible for authors to experiment so freely. It was the combination of the two, the message and the medium, that extended horizons and generated the sense of change (**77**). Yet it was this same sense that makes the published material such an unreliable source. Protestant pamphlet literature can tell us a lot about the themes of interest and how the dialogue between the various religious parties progressed, but it is not a transparent historical account. The Reformation was a war of words, a struggle to capture the affections of public opinion, and quite often it is difficult to determine where the rhetoric ends and the historical reality begins.

Words were important, but they were not the only means of expression. One of the more recent trends in Reformation historiography, and one which Scribner himself helped to pioneer, is the study of the different forms and methods of communication used to articulate ideas of reform. The value of images, for instance, was known to the medieval church, but the evangelical propagandists were the first to employ pictures and illustrations so effectively in the service of the faith. Imagery was used to fashion a public understanding of the movement. In the early years, the basic evangelical woodcut served this function (**85, 125**). Later in the century, the confessional image was fine-tuned in order to leave the viewer with an unambiguous idea of how both the faith and the church should be understood. This type of published imagery proved especially useful in the iconography of the emerging Protestant state (**22, 91**). At times word and image might intersect, as with the early woodcuts, where a simple verse would spell out the meaning of a picture. Similarly, authors might blur different literary genres in order to indoctrinate Reformation theology.

A good example of this was the run of popular astrological literature, much of it published by Protestant pastors, which made use of word and image, the secular and the spiritual, to get the point across (**28, 136**). No doubt future research will follow up other lines of association.

More dynamic methods of expression would include the use of ritual. Religious rituals in this age are usually associated with the Catholic Church, and there is no doubt that it was a type of religious 'language' more readily exploited by the Counter-Reformation. But it played a role in Protestant culture as well. In the beginning, as the evangelical movement took hold, Catholic ritual was inverted, turned on its head and mocked and divested of meaning. Later, when the Reformation church needed to create an identity of its own, ritual was refashioned to establish boundaries between confessional cultures (**62, 88**). The divisions were fine, especially those between the Lutherans and the Calvinists, but Protestant ritual proved to be an important means of expression. Above all it was dynamic, manifest in time and place and subject to manipulation. This was important, for the evangelical movement gathered much of its energy from the locations where it evolved.

(iv) Social locations

When historians speak of the social location of the German Reformation, it is usually with reference to the urban commune. No other location has been better researched than the cities. The urban Reformation was a central theme on the historiographical agenda when *The German Reformation* first appeared, and while it no longer dominates as it once did, the topic has continued to generate massive amounts of literature. Indeed, the sheer range of material has made it difficult to offer generalisations. As a consequence, instead of speaking in all-purpose terms about a single urban Reformation that took place in Germany, recent surveys have tended to identify dominant types or patterns of urban development and thus divide the discussion into analytical categories (**19, 47, 60, 108**). In the cities, the context of development was influenced by a range of factors, from local politics and geography to the social and economic relations in the commune. To offer an example, the Reformation movement in the smaller territorial towns, where local politics was subject to the will of the neighbouring prince, was different in kind to the movements that took shape in the imperial cities, where the city councils were essentially sovereign powers. In the former, the process of reform was a dialogue between the town authorities (or a distinct group in the town) and the local lord. Tensions within the commune could be complex, and there were moments of resistance and rebellion, but in the end the territorial prince would determine the course of events. In the imperial cities, in contrast, while the overlord was the Emperor himself, the more critical social and political considerations were closer to home, and as a consequence the introduction of the Reformation often took shape as part of the dialogue between the various contending sovereign interests in the urban commune. Councils could be divided between evangelicals and Catholics, while different social groups in the city (ruling patriarchs, wealthy merchants, guild members, day labourers) agitated for and against evolving notions of religious reform. It was a complex landscape.

And yet, even when we take all of the historical variety on board, there are enough common features to the urban Reformation to think of it as a distinct historical phenomenon. This becomes especially apparent when we look beneath the surface details and examine events over the long term. For instance, recent research has continued to investigate how both the evangelical movement and the formal institutionalisation of reform should be understood in relation to the social and political traditions of medieval urban Germany. It is important to recognise that the urban evangelical movement did not emerge *ex nihilo*; civic life was already subject to many of the forces of change (i.e. anticlericalism, civic communalism, the rise of the princely state) that would later take shape with the Reformation (**8, 26, 33**). Similarly, although the principles of evangelical theology ultimately fashioned a type of urban religion profoundly different in kind from medieval Catholicism, the culture of civic Protestantism was

77

also the natural legacy of urban developments (**48**). In the cities, the Reformation can thus be understood as both a catalyst for change and a conductor for forces long at work. Recent research has tried to emphasise its dual nature, in particular with reference to relations of power, tracing how the added element of religious change affected traditional notions of social and political order (**144**).

A fairly recent growth-industry in Reformation history has been the study of the movement in the rural setting. These days, much more is known about the course of events in the countryside, and we also have a better understanding of how the parishioners actually perceived the movement. The Reformation is no longer viewed as an event which occurred on the margins of village society and was then forced on the parishioners from above. Historians now view the rural setting as closely tied to the early Reformation, both as a context for development and as an imagined community for the grounding of the faith (**5, 9**). This change of perspective has been strengthened by recent research. On the one hand, modern studies of the political history of the rural commune have made it clear that these local societies were home to sophisticated cultures of rule (**6, 148**). On the eve of the Reformation, many rural communes functioned more or less as sovereign political communities, and it was only natural that the village elite would be interested in a reform of the local church when the opportunity arose. On the other hand, our knowledge of parish religion has improved over the last few decades, especially our appreciation of ecclesiological affairs (i.e. the founding and the maintenance of the parish church or the appointment of clergy), and it is clear that many rural communities in Germany had a long tradition of involvement in local religious affairs (**38**).

In a similar manner to their urban counterparts, the rural parishioners imagined religious reform at the level of the worshipping community, and that is why the idea of Reformation was so deeply rooted in the parish commune. Much progress in this area has been made in the last few years, and yet important questions remain. For instance, our knowledge of parish religion as it was practised at the local level in the late-medieval period remains very sketchy.

Yet without this essential background we can only speculate on the impact of the Reformation on the parish mind. Similarly, our interest in the rural movement often ends with the Peasants' War of 1525. But the rural Reformation was much more than this event, and historians will continue to have a difficult time assessing the effect of Protestant reform in the countryside unless we develop a long-term perspective. There have been a few recent studies of the rural Reformation over the course of the century, but more research is required before a general picture can emerge (**27, 137**).

One of the dangers in associating a historical movement too closely with certain contexts of social or political development is that it can impose a sense of order on the past which was not evident at the time. We should keep this in mind when we speak in general terms about the urban or the rural Reformations. For every parishioner who imagined reform taking shape within the parameters of the rural parish or urban commune, there was his or her counterpart who imagined it in much less local or familiar terms. Problems of this kind are unavoidable in any discussion of the relationship between the Reformation and the German people (**57**). The range of social categories was very broad, from herdsmen and shoemakers to defrocked clergy and provincial nobility. Similar concerns can be raised with reference to the notions of location. Without doubt, the features of the urban and rural environments left a powerful imprint on the nature of reform, but to speak of a circumscribed location can overlook the diversity it contains (locations within locations) and that, in turn, can easily distort our view. Not all of this is historical guesswork, for there are plenty of sources left behind which testify to differences of opinion and alternative notions of community within a distinct type of reform movement.

The rural Reformation, for instance, ran parallel to the outbreak of the Peasants' War, and there was a very close association between the two movements. Now and again we can see the shared concerns of the communal Reformation come to the surface in the peasant manifestos; but this was a revolution with more on its mind than just a reform of the parish church, and there is little doubt that the great plurality of opinion, some of it extremely radical in nature, divided the peasant communities as much as it provided a sense of common purpose (**7, 119**). Even more divisive, and much more enduring, were the ideas of reform developed by the Anabaptists. These religious groups could evolve in a great variety of locations, yet their ideas of reform and their notions of social order often ran counter to the interests of the broader community. The Anabaptists parted company with many of the main tenets of Reformation teaching. Both their religious views and their ideas of secular relations were a direct threat to the notion of the *corpus Christianum* as it was evolving in Protestant thought (**42, 79, 93, 129, 132**). It was a different sense of community, with a different context of development in mind.

(v) Politics and the Reformation

At every level of governance, from the urban parishes and rural communes to the imperial stage, the reform of religion quickly became a sensitive political issue. In the communes, as Scribner observed, the dialogue revolved around the proper meaning of civic righteousness and the extent to which the principles of the evangelical faith could be integrated into traditions of rule. Research on this theme continues, with some recent studies looking more closely at how the ruling elite in the cities and the parishes manipulated the language of Reformation to consolidate existing political relations (**27, 144**). In addition to this tradition of research there is now a renewed interest in the relationship between religious reform and the rise of the early modern state. Historians are once again devoting more time to the German territories, with more or less the same questions in mind that inspired the work on urban events. In what ways were the principles of evangelical theology related to the theory and praxis of rule? How did the introduction of the Reformation affect existing relations of rule? One thing seems fairly certain, and that is that Protestant theology could provide important ideological support for the evolving state. In the view of Lutheran reformers such as Philip Melanchthon (who derived many of his ideas from Erasmus), the Protestant prince had been appointed by God to watch over the earthly church and the salvation of its people (**34, 64–5**). In such a model, there is very little to separate the secular and the spiritual spheres of rule, and very little to distinguish between the realms of church and state. Of course, infusing politics with religious ideas could also create serious tensions, as both practical politics and theories of resistance would prove (**35, 114: 390–433**). But on the whole the Reformation invested the territorial rulers with considerable additional powers of rule. Not only was the prince responsible for the earthly welfare of the subject population; he now watched over their spiritual welfare as well, and this meant he had the right – the divine right – to oversee religious affairs. As some surveys of the Reformation in the German territories have recently illustrated, this change in status could have profound implications for the exercise and application of rule (**18, 29, 145**).

Although political history has fallen out of favour in recent times, it is now firmly back on the historiographical agenda. This is fortunate, for it is especially important in the study of the Reformation, where the exercise of rule was so crucial. Historians continue to analyse the points of intersection between the evangelical movement and traditional relations of power, not only to illustrate how the new religion could unsettle things, but to explain how matters of the spirit could have such a profound influence on worldly affairs (**25**). Once the institutionalisation of the Reformation began, it necessarily became a direct dialogue between religious ideas and the realities of political life. We have already seen how this could work to the advantage of the secular rulers, but the political systems which emerged in Protestant Germany were often shaped by a very complex array of interests, and it did not always go smoothly for the ruling elite.

Relations between the Protestant clergy and the secular authorities were often very volatile and tense. In the beginning, there was no clear idea of the new spheres of power or the structures of rule. Many clergymen, among them leading reformers such as Martin Bucer, Martin Chemnitz, and Matthias Flacius Illyricus, questioned the sovereignty of the urban authorities in their efforts to preserve the rights of the church (**17, 114**). The conflict of interest between the secular powers could be just as intense. In the imperial cities, religious reform often polarised relations between the ruling elite. City councils sought to preserve traditional structures of government, while local guilds and communal associations were often more interested in change. And as these internal tensions threatened urban stability, the possibility of intervention by neighbouring powers (princes, bishops or indeed the Emperor himself) made the context of domestic relations even more complex (**10, 107: 78–123**). Some of the most tense and fragile situations arose in the territories where the ruler attempted to see through a Second Reformation and replace the Lutheran faith with a form of Calvinism. By the latter decades of the century, notions of religious identity were explicitly interwoven with ideologies of rule. Any threat to the faith was necessarily a hazard to political livelihood. As the example of Brandenburg illustrates, confessional politics of this kind could alienate the subject population at all levels and present the sovereign with serious threat to rule (**87**). One Reformation was enough for most people.

The effect of confessional change on political relations had profound and lasting consequences for the development of the German Nation. Germany was never a consolidated monarchy in the traditional sense. Throughout the early modern period it remained a fragile confederacy of territorial powers. There was a hierarchy of rule, with the elected Emperor at the summit, but in terms of real power, sovereignty was in the hands of the princes and the imperial cities (**118, 143**). German politics had thus always been a matter of forming the most advantageous alliance. With the Reformation, the rules of power politics were rewritten. Religious affiliation could now determine the fate of a secular territory.

First affected were the imperial cities. Once a city council decided to introduce the Protestant faith, the framework of political relations changed immediately. Instead of being the overlord and protector of the city, the Catholic Emperor became a threat to local liberties. In addition, every neighbouring prince, bishop, territorial power, and imperial city, if true to the Catholic faith, were *ipso facto* a threat to local security. The only sure method of defence was to create a military alliance, and this is what most of the major Lutheran powers tried to effect with the formation of the Schmalkaldic League (1531) (**10, 37, 111**). With the establishment of this military alliance it was the German princes, rather than the cities, who determined the fate of the Reformation movement. In truth, most of the princes were rather slow to take a public stand in the Luther affair; the high-profile activities of Saxony and Hesse have overshadowed the general sense of reluctance (**146**). But once the confessional issue could no longer be avoided and the territorial rulers were forced by circumstance to take a public stand, the political divisions in the German lands began to multiply. This was especially apparent after the Peace of Augsburg (1555), when the formal settlement provided a legal basis for Lutheran reform. In the latter decades of the century, the process of confessional polarisation completely transformed the political landscape of the German Nation (**90, 96, 109**).

(vi) Varieties and perspectives of Reformation

In his discussion of the varieties of Reformation, Scribner singled out the issues which divided the reformers and set the evangelical movement on divergent paths. In the beginning it was primarily a case of questions relating to the speed and the extent of reform; later in the century the points of disagreement became more theologically complex and confessional culture became more and more intolerant. The reason these conflicts lasted the century was due to the fact that there was never a solitary and uncontested ideal of Reformation, not even within the individual Protestant traditions. Variety was rife, with many of the discrepencies touching on matters of fundamental theological importance, from the nature of the evangelical church to the proper interpretation of scripture (**124**).

Yet even with all of this variety in mind, there are models of the Reformation that can capture essential features of the event. It depends on the perspective of the historian.

The closer we get to the religious ideas at the heart of the movement, for instance, the easier it becomes to isolate the principles of thought that dominated theological discourse. Theology may not be the most reliable guide to public perception, but it was the language the reformers used in their efforts to define the movement (**69**). Similarly, the closer we get to the political events associated with the Reformation, the easier it becomes to construct a traditional historical narrative, with a point of origin, a series of fateful events and a number of possible endings. The Reformation was, after all, a social and political phenomenon, not just a shift in religious thinking, and the progress of the movement can be measured against the chronology of human affairs (**122**). Moving farther away from the local details can offer yet another perspective on the movement, and another means of reducing the variety to a manageable whole. In German historiography, the paradigm of confessionalisation has been the most influential example of this type of approach. With confessionalisation, religion remains important to interpretation, but primarily due to its role as a type of guiding logic for the evolution of the broader framework of affairs (**97–8, 109**). To cite a recent synthesis:

> The confessional hypothesis focuses both on the cultural, intellectual, social, and political functions of religion and confession within the early modern social order and on the confessions' roles as spurs and barriers to the emergence of modernity. These are two sides of the historical paradigm we call "confessionalization". It holds that the late sixteenth-century emergence of confessions was one of the key events in early modernization, because the doctrinal and organizational strengthening of the churches became a powerful prelude to political and social reorganization in the following era (109, pp. 642–3).

With this model, the Reformation is thus placed at the forefront of historical developments, though not without a degree of distortion, for there is little to distinguish secular and spiritual developments. Moreover, it becomes very difficult to make room for the details and dynamics of local history, especially when they challenge or contradict the broader paradigm. But there is no doubt that the idea of confessionalisation captures a central feature of the age.

In recent years historians have continued to concentrate on the actual impact of the Reformation. Usually this is done by looking at a fairly general aspect of the movement, such as the relationship between evangelical teaching and parish beliefs or the effect of the Protestant Church on the moral conduct of the parishioners, and measuring the final results against the early expectations of the reformers. In the English-language world, this debate has been couched in terms of success and failure, and it has often resulted in interpretations placed at opposite ends of the spectrum (**94**). Recent investigations of religious life in the rural parishes of Germany have suggested that the Protestant faith had a very limited impact, at least during the first century of reform. Local religion was not purged of popular beliefs or what the reformers termed Catholic superstitions, medieval traditions of worship remained more or less intact, while the tensions between the clergy and the parishioners increased as the new church struggled to find a place in local systems of rule (**27, 121, 123**). Others studies have challenged this bleak picture, arguing that by the end of the century the reformers accomplished many of their pedagogical goals, especially in larger imperial cities such as Strasbourg (**66**).

Discrepancies exist, and once again it is primarily a question of perspective. We know, for instance, that the course of reform did effect a process of structural and ideological change in the German lands at the level of rule. This age experienced the rise of the confessional state, Protestant and Catholic alike, with all aspects of public life, from the systems of rule and institutions of governance to general notions of identity and private belief, becoming the objects of deliberate and calculated reform (**58**). However, the objectives of the state were not simply imposed on a subject population and then translated into historical reality. The Reformation was a continuous dialogue between the ideals of the Protestant authorities and the realities of local life, and the most representative picture of the past is probably one that does not imagine the process in terms of opposites,

85

such as success or failure, but rather in a more ambiguous sense of dialogue and exchange (**43**). Protestantism did not transform the thoughts and behaviour of the German people in the way the reformers had planned, and yet there is little doubt that the culture and society of Reformation Germany was different in kind from the medieval age.

It is difficult for historians to assess changes in mental attitudes or shifts in collective perspective. Protestantism was a different religion from medieval Catholicism, but as has been suggested above, that did not necessarily equate to a new type of religious culture at the level of historical experience. In the parishes, the reality was more about shades of understanding than stark contrasts. Only at the level of public discourse, where group identity was fashioned and articulated, were the confessional distinctions clearly projected. The most obvious shifts in perception were associated with the culture of the church. Over the course of the century Protestant historians reinterpreted the history of Christianity to accommodate, and to legitimate, the emergence of the Reformation (**44, 54**). A narrative of Protestant Church history came into being, with its own unique interpretation of sacred history, its own inspirational figures, and its own distinct notions of how the Christian community had evolved over time (**68**). And there was no room for compromise, as both Catholics and Protestants condemned and rejected the religion of the other side. Scholars, once joined by philosophical schools or hermeneutical techniques, now parted company on the basis of religion; clergymen, once a common estate with a common perspective, now viewed the world from different theological standpoints; secular rulers, always looking for ways to enhance their control over the subject population, now defined their claims to sovereignty by borrowing from the language of confessionalisation (**4, 89, 98, 106**).

The extent to which perspectives of this kind filtered down to the general public is still a matter of debate among historians. In general, abstract notions of religious history and confessional identity took generations to make headway. More direct forms of cultural contact, in contrast, such as the displays associated with religious ritual or the rites of passage in the church, had more of an immediate effect;

but even in these matters the distinctions were very fine. Future studies of the impact of the Reformation on German culture will likely emphasise the subtle shifts in perspective over a relatively long period of time rather than look for abrupt changes in insight or awareness. By the end of the sixteenth century there are signs of a nascent Protestant culture in Europe, but it has to be carefully reconstructed from the details of the past (**78, 127, 128: 323–45**).

Whether there was such a thing as a Protestant society is the other central question bound up with the issues of impact and effect. As Scribner observed, the claims that have been made about the impact of the Reformation have often been extreme. And when we examine just how far the movement reached in the social world of the sixteenth century, it is easy to understand why such claims have been made. It is also easy to understand why the Reformation has been so strongly associated with the modern age, for many of the traits associated with early Protestantism are still with us today (**31**). As in many aspects of this history, however, the role of the Reformation appears to have been rather ambiguous. There is no doubt that Protestant reform introduced significant social innovations and new patterns to Christian life, including the reform of the welfare system, new approaches to education, a subtle change of relations in the household (between spouses and between whole families), and, of course, a transformation of public worship and the constitution of the church (**104**). Yet many of these changes were already in train before the Reformation took hold, and while the movement undoubtedly accelerated the process and added its own distinct impression, timelines of social change in early modern Germany did not necessarily run parallel with confessional developments. This is not to question the importance of the event, just to point out, as recent research has done, that assessing the impact of the Reformation on the social world is a very complex issue, for it was not a straightforward matter of transforming intentions into historical experience.

By way of example we might conclude by referring to the work that has been done on the impact of reform on the role of women in German society. Women in the Protestant world

87

remained subordinate to a patriarchal ideology, and even more so in some contexts (such as urban artisanal culture, for instance) where the evangelical notions of Christian morality elevated the authority of the husband. At the same time, however, evangelical theology could allow more of an active role for women in the religious community (Anabaptism in particular), both in the home and the church, and while the Reformation dissolved the culture of religious orders, new social possibilities did evolve in its place, many of which grew out of the secular reforms relating to marriage and education (**53, 100, 142**). The effect of reform was unequal, in this matter as in many others. Today historians face the same challenge identified by Scribner sixteen years ago when he advised historians of the Reformation 'to sift out what was original from what was not, to compare projected ideals with reality, and to discern what was an ambivalent change with a two-edged effect'. The Reformation left a complex legacy, and modern research must keep the balance in view.

Select Bibliography

This is intended to provide a basic reading list of recent works in English, and of some important recent works in German, which are listed at the end of each section. The sections correspond to the chapter divisions, and also serve the purpose of providing references to the works on which I have relied throughout. The 'Miscellaneous' section at the end contains largely collected works and reference items. Place of publication is London, unless otherwise stated.

General Surveys, Interpretations

[1] A. G. Dickens, *The German Nation and Martin Luther* (1974). First recent work to examine the socio-political context of the Reformation; coined the phrase 'the Reformation was an urban event'.

[2] A. G. Dickens and J. Tonkin, *A Historiography of the Reformation* (Cambridge, Mass.: Harvard University Press; Oxford: Basil Blackwell, 1985). Comprehensive survey, from earliest sixteenth-century writings up to modern social historical approaches.

[3] W. Monter, *Ritual, Myth and Magic in Early Modern Europe* (Brighton, 1983). Misleadingly titled, but excellent on piety, 'superstition' and the authoritarian attitude to religion (from both Protestant and Catholic).

[4] S. E. Ozment, *The Age of Reform 1250–1550* (New Haven, 1980). Very good survey of theological and intellectual antecedents of the Reformation. Takes account, if patchily, of social historical approaches, but dismissive of 'popular religion'.

[5] S. E. Ozment (ed.), *Reformation Europe: A Guide to Research* (St Louis, Miss., 1982). A guide for the advanced student, concentrated heavily on Germany and Switzerland, but contains some very informative essays and bibliographies.

[6] M. Mullett, *Radical Religious Movements in Early Modern Europe* (1980). Excellent attempt to break out of traditional categories,

89

tracing 'radical religion' from Hus to Quakers in five thought-provoking thematic chapters.

[7] B. M. G. Reardon, *Religious Thought in the Reformation* (1981). Old-fashioned approach which equates 'religious thought' with theology, but a very useful survey of Reformation doctrine.

[8] R. W. Scribner, 'Is there a Social History of the Reformation?', *Social History*, II (1977), 483–505. Discusses approaches to social history of the Reformation, especially West German debates with marxist interpretations.

[9] R. W. Scribner, 'Religion, Society and Culture: Reorientating the Reformation', *History Workshop*, 14 (1982), 2–22. Discusses recent views on Reformation, popular culture and popular religion.

[10] R. W. Scribner, 'Interpreting Religion in Early Modern Europe', *European Studies Review*, XIII (1983), 89–105. Examines approaches to history of religion which use sociology and social anthropology to interpret Reformation as part of long-term cultural change.

[11] P. Blickle, *Die Reformation im Reich* (Stuttgart, 1982). Brief overview, containing the author's interpretation of the Reformation as a 'communal Reformation'. See also [36].

[12] K. von Greyerz, 'Stadt und Reformation: Stand und Aufgaben der Forschung', *Archiv für Reformationsgeschichte*, LXXVI (1985). Perceptive survey of literature on the urban Reformation, mostly works to appear since 1980.

[13] B. Moeller, *Deutschland im Zeitalter der Reformation* (Göttingen, 1977). Brief but stimulating synthesis of recent trends to that date, especially tries to incorporate social historical material.

[14] B. Moeller, 'Problems of Reformation Research' in [65]. Classic 1965 article, which called for a more historical and less purely theological approach to the Reformation.

[15] R. Wohlfeil, *Einführung in die Geschichte der deutschen Reformation* (Munich, 1982). Stimulating analytical discussion of concepts and approaches to Reformation, especially good on social historical approach and on recent controversies.

Religion and Reformation

See also [136], [141]

[16] J. Bossy, 'The Mass as a Social Institution 1200–1700', *Past and Present*, 100 (1983), 29–61. Discusses the significance of the Mass, though concentrates only on its central ceremony, the canon.

[17] H. Bornkamm, *Luther in Mid-Career 1521–1530* (1983). Magisterial study of Luther, combining lucid exposition of his theology with historical perspective. For later period of Luther's life, see [89].

[18] W. A. Christian, *Apparitions in Late Medieval and Renaissance Spain* (Princeton, 1981). Important anthropological view of late-medieval religion; along with [19] one of the most important works of recent years for understanding religion as social phenomenon.

[19] W. A. Christian, *Local Religion in Sixteenth Century Spain* (Princeton, 1981).

[20] J. Delumeau, *Catholicism between Luther and Voltaire* (1977). Important for 'christianisation' thesis.

[21] K. von Greyerz (ed.), *Religion and Society in Early Modern Europe* (1985). Proceedings of recent conference on popular religion, with important papers from international scholars.

[22] J. Huizinga, *The Waning of the Middle Ages* (1955). Classic study on 'decayed' religion at end of middle ages, though written from perspective of cultural elites.

[23] R. E. Lerner, 'Medieval Prophecy and Religious Dissent', *Past and Present*, 72 (1976), 3–24. Places Luther in tradition of medieval prophecy.

[24] B. McGinn, *Visions of the End: Apocalyptic Visions in the Middle Ages* (New York, 1979). Valuable collection of documents on the apocalyptic tradition, unfortunately stops at 1500. See also [31], [34].

[25] B. Moeller, 'Religious Life in Germany on the Eve of the Reformation', in G. Strauss (ed.), *Pre-Reformation Germany* (1972), 13–42. Originally published 1965, arguing for strength of piety on eve of Reformation.

[26] F. Oakley, 'Religious and Ecclesiastical Life on the Eve of the Reformation', in (5). Useful short survey with excellent bibliography.

[27] F. Oakley, *The Western Church in the Later Middle Ages* (Ithaca, 1979). Perceptive and balanced survey, especially good on piety, reform.

[28] H. A. Oberman, *Luther: Man between God and Devil* (1985). Best biography of Luther of recent times for seeing him in religious perspective of his age.

[29] H. A. Oberman, *Masters of the Reformation* (Cambridge, 1981). Places the Reformation in medieval and south German perspective.

[30] S. E. Ozment, *The Reformation in the Cities* (New Haven, 1975). Good on the appeal of the evangelical message, suggestive on the urban Reformation.

91

[31] M. Reeves, *Joachim of Fiore and the Prophetic Future* (1976). Important on Joachimism's influence on the Reformation apocalyptic tradition.

[32] L. Rothkrug, *Religious Practices and Collective Perceptions: Hidden Homologies in the Renaissance and Reformation* (Waterloo, Ontario, 1980). Stimulating but controversial interpretation of popular religion and Reformation. For a critique see [9], [10].

[33] R. W. Scribner, 'Ritual and Popular Religion in Catholic Germany at the time of the Reformation', *Journal of Ecclesiastical History*, xxxv (1984), 47–77. Defines 'popular religion' in terms of liturgical practices.

[34] W. E. Peuckert, *Die grosse Wende. Das apokalyptische Säculum und Luther* (Hamburg, 1948). Much neglected, but important study of the apocalyptic dimension of the Reformation.

[35] R. W. Scribner, 'Luther-Legenden des 16. Jahrhunderts', in G. Vogler (ed.), *Martin Luther. Leben, Werk, Wirkung* (Berlin, 1983). Examines myths built around Luther from beginning of the Reformation.

[35a] R. W. Scribner, 'Incombustible Luther: the Image of the Reformer in Early Modern Germany', *Past and Present*, 110(1986), 38–68. Discusses persistence of the view of Luther as saint and miracle-worker until the eighteenth century.

The Reformation as Evangelical Movement

See also [6], [8], [11], [12], [15], [29], [30], [134], [137], [138], [144]

[36] P. Blickle, *The Revolution of 1525* (Baltimore, 1981). Sees the Peasants' War as the 'revolution of the common man'. See also [5], [9], [10], [11].

[37] M. U. Chrisman, 'Lay Response to the Protestant Reformation in Germany, 1520–1528', in [126]. Examines lay pamphlets in support of Reformation.

[38] H. J. Cohn, 'Anticlericalism in the German Peasants' War', *Past and Present*, 83 (1979), 3–31. Argues importance of socio-economic hostility to clergy.

[39] R. G. Cole, 'The Reformation Pamphlet and Communication Processes', in [129]. Argues for importance of printing in communicating Reformation ideas.

[40] R. G. Cole, 'Reformation Printers: Unsung Heroes', *Sixteenth Century Journal*, xv (1984), 327–39. Emphasises the importance of printers as supporters of the Reformation.

[41] E. M. Eisenstein, *The Printing Press as an Agent of Change* (Cambridge, 1979). Perceptive if rather over-argued case for cultural impact of printing.

[42] J. M. Kittelson, 'Humanism and the Reformation in Germany', *Central European History*, IX (1976), 303–22. Points out continuing importance of humanism for Reformation.

[43] S. E. Ozment, 'The Social History of the Reformation: What can we learn from Pamphlets?', in [129]. Argues for importance of pamphlets as a historical source. See [30], [113] for examples, [46], [127] for criticism of this approach.

[44] R. W. Scribner, 'The Reformation as a Social Movement', in [127]. Tries to define meaning of 'social movement', using central German examples.

[45] R. W. Scribner, *For the Sake of Simple Folk. Popular Propaganda for the German Reformation* (Cambridge, 1981). Study of broadsheet propaganda as a means of spreading evangelical ideas to the illiterate and semi-illiterate.

[46] R. W. Scribner, 'Oral Culture and the Diffusion of Reformation Ideas', *History of European Ideas*, V (1984). Argues that role of printing has been overestimated and that oral communication should be given more attention in spread of Reformation.

[47] R. W. Scribner, 'Practice and Principle in the German Towns: Preachers and People', in [124]. Analysis of role and social profile of leading Reformation preachers.

[48] H. J. Cohn, 'Reformatorische Bewegung und Anticlericalismus in Deutschland und England', in [127]. Illuminating comparison of anticlerical feeling in German and English Reformations.

[49] H. Fast, 'Reformation durch Provokation. Predigtstörungen in den ersten Jahren der Reformation in der Schweiz', in [102]. Discusses use of public provocation to further reform.

[50] B. Moeller, 'Einige Bemerkungen zum Thema: Predigten in reformatorischen Flugschriften', in [129]. Points out importance of sermon for dissemination of Reformation.

[51] B. Moeller, 'Stadt und Buch. Bemerkungen zur Struktur der reformatorischen Bewegung in Deutschland', in [127]. Argues importance of printing for spread of Reformation, though position qualified by [50].

[52] B. Moeller, 'Was wurde in der Frühzeit der Reformation in den deutschen Städten gepredigt?', *Archiv für Reformationsgeschichte*, LXXV (1984), 176–93. Studies collections of printed sermons to

discover what was preached in the towns during the early years of the evangelical movement.

[53] H. J. Goertz, 'Aufstand gegen den Priester. Antiklerikalismus und reformatorische Bewegung', in P. Blickle (ed.), *Bauer, Reich und Reformation* (Stuttgart, 1982), 182–209. Argues importance of anticlericalism for reform movements, especially for radical tradition.

Social Location of the Reformation

See also [12], [36], [40], [134], [137], [143], [144]

[54] T. A. Brady, *Ruling Class, Regime and Reformation at Strasbourg 1520–1555* (Leiden, 1978). Study of socio-economic influence on urban reform, underpinned by excellent analysis of social and political system in Strasbourg.

[55] T. A. Brady, 'Social History', in [5]. Overview of tasks for social historical study of reform movements.

[56] P. Broadhead, 'Politics and Expediency in the Augsburg Reformation', in [124]. This and following item show importance of political calculation in urban Reformation.

[57] P. Broadhead, 'Popular Pressure for Reform in Augsburg, 1524–1534', in [127].

[58] M. U. Chrisman, *Strasbourg and the Reform* (New Haven, 1967). First of the current wave of works on the urban Reformation.

[59] M. U. Chrisman, 'Women and the Reformation in Strasbourg 1490–1530', *Archiv für Reformationsgeschichte*, LXIII (1972), 143–67. First careful examination of the role of women in Reformation not just concerned with 'famous women'.

[60] H. J. Grimm, *Lazarus Spengler. A Lay Leader of the Reformation* (Columbus, Ohio, 1978). Rewarding biography of a central figure of the Nuremberg Reformation.

[61] H. J. Hillerbrand, 'The Reformation and the German Peasants' War', in [125]. Argues that religion played only a minor role in peasant grievances.

[62] J. Irwin, 'Society and the Sexes', in [5]. Useful survey of the rather sparse work on the role of women in the Reformation. Shows how much work is still to be done.

[63] S. Karant-Nunn, *Luther's Pastors: the Reformation in the Ernestine Countryside*, Transactions of the American Philosophical Society, 69 (1979). Examines effectiveness of Lutheranism in rural areas through investigation of the ministers implementing reform.

[64] B. Moeller, 'The German Humanists and the Beginning of the Reformation', in [65]. First published 1965, argues for importance of humanists for initial reception of the Reformation.

[65] B. Moeller, *Imperial Cities and the Reformation* (Philadelphia, 1972). Classic essay from 1962 which set off current discussion of the social dimension of Reformation. Here with other important essays by same author, see [14], [64].

[66] R. W. Scribner, 'Civic Unity and the Reformation in Erfurt', *Past and Present*, 66 (1975), 29–60. Examines importance of social conflict in fate of the Reformation in a major European town; critical of Moeller [65] for underestimating social conflict.

[67] R. W. Scribner, 'Memorandum on the Appointment of a Preacher in Speyer, 1538', *Bulletin of the Institute of Historical Research*, XLVIII (1975), 248–55. Why Reformation was postponed in Speyer for economic and political reasons.

[68] R. W. Scribner, 'Why was there no Reformation in Cologne?', *Bulletin of the Institute of Historical Research*, XLIX (1976), 217–41. Social and political pressures, internal and external, which prevented growth of a reform movement.

[69] R. W. Scribner, 'Reformation, Carnival and the World Turned Upside-down', *Social History*, III (1977), 303–29. Use of carnival and popular culture to spread Reformation.

[70] J. C. Stalnaker, 'Residenzstadt und Reformation: Religion, Politics and Social Policy in Hesse, 1509–46', *Archiv für Reformationsgeschichte*, LXIV (1973), 113–46. One of the few studies of a residence-town outside south Germany (Marburg) examining socio-political dimensions of reform.

[71] V. Press, 'Adel, Reich und Reformation' in [127]. Excellent overview of response of nobility to Reformation in sixteenth century; with English summary.

Politics and the Reformation

See also [1], [6], [36], [54], [56], [66] to [71], [89], [137]

[72] T. A. Brady, 'Patricians, Nobles, Merchants: Internal Tensions and Solidarities in South German Ruling Classes at the Close of the Middle Ages', in [126]. Useful overview of oligarchies.

[73] T. A. Brady, 'Princes' Reformation versus Urban Liberty: Strasbourg and the Restoration in Wurttemberg, 1534', in [128].

[74] P. N. Brooks, '*Visitator*: Luther as Visitor', in P. N. Brooks (ed.), *Seven-headed Luther* (Oxford, 1983). On Luther's role in the first Saxon church visitation.

[75] W. D. J. Cargill-Thompson, *The Political Thought of Martin Luther* (Hassocks, 1984). Surveys main lines of Luther's political thought.

[76] C. R. Friedrichs, 'Citizens or Subjects? Urban Conflict in Early Modern Germany', in [126]. On tendency of ruling authorities to treat citizens as subjects and to behave as sovereign authorities.

[77] K. von Greyerz, *The late city Reformation in Germany: the Case of Colmar 1522–1638* (Wiesbaden, 1980). Singles out typology of towns with 'late' Reformations.

[78] H. Hopfl, *The Christian Polity of John Calvin* (Cambridge, 1982). Development of Calvin's views on government within practical context of Geneva.

[79] G. R. Potter, *Zwingli* (Cambridge, 1976). Fine and most recent biography of Zwingli in English.

[80] G. R. Potter, *Huldrych Zwingli* (1978). Excellent collection of documents to accompany [79].

[81] H. C. Rublack, 'Political and Social Norms in Urban Communities in the Holy Roman Empire', in K. von Greyerz (ed.), *Religion, Politics and Social Protest. Three Studies on Early Modern Germany* (1985). Overview of political and social norms, and their relationship to urban reform.

[82] B. Scribner and G. Benecke (eds), *The German Peasant War 1525: New Viewpoints* (1979). Collection of translated articles from the best and recent (to 1978) German scholarship.

[83] H. Schilling, 'The Reformation in the Hanseatic Cities', *Sixteenth Century Journal*, xv (1983), 443–56. Argues for a 'Hansa-city' Reformation.

[84] W. J. Wright, 'The Homberg Synod and Philip of Hesse's Plan for a new Church-State Settlement', *Sixteen Century Journal*, iv (1973), 23–46.

[85] P. Blickle, *Deutsche Untertanen: ein Widerspruch* (Munich, 1981). Argues that there is a long tradition of peasant protest and political struggle to achieve autonomy.

[86] M. Heckel, *Deutschland im konfessionellen Zeitalter* (Göttingen, 1983). On Protestant confessional politics and legal implications of reform in the Empire.

Varieties of Reformation

See also [6], [7], [49], [53], [78] to [80], [123], [135], [139]

[87] C. P. Clasen, *Anabaptism. A Social History 1525–1618* (1972). First extended social analysis of the Anabaptists.

[88] M. U. Edwards, *Luther and the False Brethren* (Stanford, 1975). Valuable study of how Luther fell out with other reformers.

[89] M. U. Edwards, *Luther's Last Battles. Politics and Polemics 1531–46* (Leiden, 1983). Excellent study of Luther's polemics in his mature years.

[90] G. Haendler, *Luther on Ministerial Office and Congregational Function* (Philadelphia, 1981) Study of how Luther's views changed 1520–4.

[91] R. Kolb, *Nikolaus von Amsdorf (1483–1565)* (Nieuwkoop, 1978). Illuminating study of Luther's disciple who tried to preserve Luther's thought as a rigid orthodoxy after 1546.

[92] J. S. Oyer, *Lutheran Reformers against Anabaptists* (The Hague, 1964). Valuable study of how the 'mainstream' reformers stigmatised the Anabaptists.

[93] C. A. Pater, *Karlstadt as the Father of the Baptist Movements: the Emergence of Lay Protestantism* (Toronto, 1984). Rescues Karlstadt's reputation as a serious evangelical thinker, and argues for his wider influence on Zwingli and the Anabaptists.

[94] J. S. Preus, *Carlstadt's Ordinaciones and Luther's Liberty. A Study of the Wittenberg Movement 1521–22* (Harvard, 1974). Study of where and how the two disagreed.

[95] G. Rupp, *Patterns of Reformation* (1969). Brief treatment of some reformers hitherto neglected in English, especially good on Karlstadt and Müntzer.

[96] J. M. Stayer and W. O. Packull (eds), *The Anabaptists and Thomas Müntzer* (Dubuque, Iowa, 1980). Translations of significant recent articles on radical reformers.

[97] J. M. Stayer, *Anabaptists and the Sword* (Lawrence, 1972). Important discussion of Anabaptist views on political authority.

[98] J. M. Stayer, 'The Anabaptists', in [5]. Sums up succinctly the state of present research.

[99] L. H. Zuck (ed.), *Christianity and Revolution. Radical Christian Testimonies 1520–1650* (Philadelphia, 1975). Selection of documents which allows the revolutionary reformed tradition to speak for itself.

[100] K. Deppermann, *Melchior Hoffman. Soziale Unruhen und apokalyptische Visionen im Zeitalter der Reformation* (Göttingen, 1979). Exemplary biography combining social history with theological analysis.

[101] H. J. Goertz (ed.), *Profiles of Radical Reformers* (Scottdale, Penn., 1982). Biographical sketches from Müntzer to Paracelsus.

[102] H. J. Goertz (ed.), *Umstrittenes Täufertum 1525–1975* (Göttingen, 1975). Important collection of revisionary essays, marking a move away from normative Lutheran assessments of the radicals.
[103] H. J. Goertz, *Die Täufer. Geschichte und Deutung* (Munich, 1980). Excellent interpretation of the role of the Anabaptists in the Reformation.

Impact of the Reformation

See also [3], [6], [9], [10], [20], [21], [32], [35], [35a], [41], [63], [136], [140], [142], [143]
[104] P. Burke, *Popular Culture in Early Modern Europe* (1978). Argues for a 'Reformation of popular culture'.
[105] M. U. Chrisman, *Lay Culture, Learned Culture. Books and Social Change in Strasbourg 1480–1599* (New Haven, 1982). Important study of impact of printing, with creation of two cultures, lay and learned.
[106] M. U. Edwards, 'Lutheran Pedagogy in Reformation Germany', *History of Education Quarterly*, XXI (1981), 471–7. Thoughtful review of [120].
[107] R. Gawthrop and G. Strauss, 'Protestantism and Literacy in Early Modern Germany', *Past and Present*, 104 (1984).
[108] R. A. Houston, 'Literacy and Society in the West 1500–1850', *Social History*, VIII (1983).
[109] S. Karant-Nunn, 'Continuity and Change. Some Effects of the Reformation on the Women of Zwickau', *Sixteenth Century Journal*, XIII (1982), 17–42.
[110] J. M. Kittelson, 'Successes and Failures in the German Reformation: the Report from Strasbourg', *Archiv für Reformationsgeschichte*, LXXIII (1983), 153–75. Criticism of [120], based on analysis of Strasbourg materials.
[111] H. Lis and C. Soly, *Poverty and Capitalism in Pre-industrial Europe* (Hassocks, 1979). Long-term study of development of treatment of the poor which sets the Reformation in perspective.
[112] R. Muchembled, 'The Witches of the Cambresis. The Acculturation of the Rural World in the Sixteenth Century', in J. Obelkevich (ed.), *Religion and the People 800–1700* (Chapel Hill, N.C., 1979), 221–76. Interprets witch persecutions as an attempt of urban elite culture to undermine rural popular culture. See also [141].

[113] S. E. Ozment, *When Fathers Ruled. Family Life in Reformation Europe* (Cambridge, Mass., 1983). A view of the Reformation's role in reaffirming the patriarchal family.

[114] T. Robisheaux, 'Peasants and Pastors: Rural Youth Control and the Reformation in Hohenlohe, 1540–1680', *Social History*, VI (1981), 281–300. A view of the triangular struggle for social control between pastors, village elders and youth.

[115] L. Roper, 'Luther: Sex, Marriage and Motherhood', *History Today*, XXXIII (1983). Assesses positive and negative effects of Luther's ideas.

[116] L. Roper, 'Going to Church and Street: Weddings in Reformation Augsburg', *Past and Present*, 106 (1985). How the Reformation changed the celebration of weddings.

[117] L. Roper, ' "Discipline and Respectability": Protestantism and the Reformation in Augsburg', *History Workshop Journal*, 19 (1985).

[118] T. M. Safley, *Let no Man Put Asunder. The Control of Marriage in the German Southwest: a Comparative Study 1550–1600* (Kirksville, Miss., 1984). Study of Protestant and Catholic marriage courts in Basel, Constance, Freiburg.

[119] G. Strauss, 'Success and Failure in the German Reformation', *Past and Present*, 67 (1975), 30–63. Uses visitation records to argue that Reformation failed to change Christian life in its territories.

[120] G. Strauss, *Luther's House of Learning. Indoctrination of the Young in the German Reformation* (Baltimore, 1978). Analyses Protestant pedagogy to argue that it was inadequate for purposes of reform.

[121] R. Muchembled, *Culture populaire et culture des élites* (Paris, 1978). Argues that elite urban culture 'acculturated' rural culture in interests of absolutist state. See [9], [10] for further discussion.

[122] B. Vogler, 'La politique scolaire entre Rhin et Moselle', *Francia*, III/IV (1975–6). Scholarly study of educational policy in Duchy of Zweibrücken, 1556–1619.

[123] B. Vogler, *Le clergé protestant rhenan au siècle de la reforme (1555–1619)* (Paris, 1976). Detailed study of position of clergy in reformed parts of Rhineland.

Miscellaneous and Addenda

[124] P. N. Brooks (ed.), *Reformation Principle and Practice. Essays in Honour of A.G. Dickens* (1980).

[125]   L. P. Buck and J. W. Zophy (eds), *The Social History of the Reformation* (Columbus, Ohio, 1872).

[126]   M. U. Chrisman and O. Grundler (eds), *Social Groups and Religious Ideas in the Sixteenth Century* (Kalamazoo, Mich., 1978).

[127]   W. J. Mommsen, P. Alter and R. W. Scribner (eds), *Stadtbürgertum und Adel in der Reformation* (Stuttgart, 1979). Contains essays in English and German (with English summaries).

[128]   I. Batori (ed.), *Städtische Gesellschaft und Reformation* (Stuttgart, 1980).

[129]   H. J. Köhler (ed.), *Flugschriften als Massenmedium der Reformationszeit* (Stuttgart, 1981).

[130]   M. Brecht and H. Ehmer, *Südwestdeutsche Reformationsgeschichte* (Stuttgart, 1984). Most recent synthesis of Reformation history of the south-west, covering present-day state of Baden-Wuerttemberg.

[131]   E. Cameron, *The Reformation of the Heretics. The Waldenses of the Alps 1480–1580* (Oxford, 1984). Study of pre-Reformation communities of the French Alps and the impact on them of the Reformation. Suggestive for German parallels.

[132]   W. Ullmann, *Principles of Government and Politics in the Middle Ages* (1974). Now classic study of the two themes in medieval government – the descending and the ascending nature of power.

[133]   H. R. Hitchcock, *German Renaissance Architecture* (Princeton, 1981). Especially useful on impact of Reformation on building and building styles.

[134]   F. Conrad, *Reformation in der bäuerlichen Gesellschaft. Zur Rezeption reformatorischer Theologie im Elsass* (Stuttgart, 1984). The first modern attempt to explore peasant reception and reaction to evangelical ideas. A splendidly suggestive study, which makes the best of limited surviving evidence.

(The following works appeared after this book was completed, and could only be briefly referred to in the text; accordingly they are commented on more fully here.)

[135]   L. J. Abray, *The People's Reformation. Magistrates, Clergy and Commons in Strasbourg 1500–1598* (Oxford, 1985). Excellent study of the varieties of reform in a major imperial city, and of the extended process required to establish a 'Lutheran' Reformation.

[136]   J. Bossy, *Christianity in the West 1400–1700* (Oxford, 1985). Scholarly and subtle argument about a 'communal' Christianity

up to 1500, replaced thereafter by an 'individualised' religion. Ignores popular religion and popular culture to present an over-idealised view of pre-Reformation religion; Reformation and Counter-Reformation seen more through a 'history of ideas' approach than through examination of their social history.

[137] T. A. Brady, *Turning Swiss. Cities and Empire 1450–1550* (Cambridge, 1985). Imaginative political study of the possibility of a 'third way' in late-medieval, early modern politics in Germany, involving free cities adopting Swiss models of collective government; although this did not have a long-term appeal, it was revived briefly by the 'communal Reformation' in south Germany. Splendidly suggestive and casts new light on political choices of imperial towns in wake of Reformation.

[138] P. Blickle, *Gemeindereformation. Die Menschen des 16. Jahrhunderts auf dem Weg zum Heil* (Munich, 1985). Fuller exposition of Blickle's thesis about a 'communal Reformation' (see also 11, 36, 137).

[139] P. Blickle (ed.), *Zwingli und Europa* (Zurich, 1985). Proceedings of 1984 conference celebrating quincentenary of Zwingli's birth; papers reflect numerous new approaches to Reformation, as well as more positive evaluation of Zwingli's importance.

[140] R. Po-Chia Hsia, *Society and Religion in Munster 1535–1618* (New Haven, 1984). Fine study of the restoration of Catholicism in Munster in the three generations following the fall of the Anabaptist Kingdom. Full of suggestive material on the emergence of 'confessionalism'.

[141] R. Muchembled, *Popular Culture and Elite Culture in France 1400–1750* (Baton Rouge, 1985). Translation of controversial 1978 work, arguing that rural 'popular culture' underwent an 'acculturation' by elite urban culture in the wake of the Counter-Reformation. For criticisms see [9, 10, 12, 21].

[142] H. Rebel, *Peasant Classes. The Bureaucratization of Property and Family Relations under Early Habsburg Absolutism 1511–1636* (Princeton, 1983). Groundbreaking study of impact of absolutist state on peasant family, with valuable sidelights on social and political aspects of Counter-Reformation in the Austrian Monarchy.

[143] L. Roper, *Work, Marriage and Sexuality: Women in Reformation Augsburg* (University of London Ph. D. Thesis, 1985). Outstanding pioneering work about how the Reformation affected the position of women, especially attempt to impose a form of 'civic righteousness' through a reformed moralism.

101

[144] P. Russell, *Lay Theology in the Reformation. Popular Pamphleteers in Southwest Germany 1521–1525* (Cambridge, 1985). Studies the works of eight lay pamphleteers, showing the mixture of theological influences from Luther and from traditional thought found in their pamphlets.

Supplementary Bibliography

In keeping with the original, this bibliography is meant to provide a basic reading list of recent works in English along with a selection of works in German that have special relevance for English-language scholarship.

[1] M. Arnold, *Handwerker als theologische Schriftsteller. Studien zu Flugschriften der frühen Reformation (1523–1525)* (Göttingen, 1990). Study of ten artisan pamphleteers and their understanding of the evangelical message.

[2] D. V. N. Bagchi, *Luther's Earliest Opponents. Catholic Controversialists 1518–1525* (Minneapolis, 1991). Examines the reaction of the Catholic theologians who first published against Luther. Emphasises the lack of unity and the need to establish authority.

[3] R. B. Barnes, *Prophecy and Gnosis. Apocalypticism in the Wake of the Lutheran Reformation* (Stanford, 1988). Survey, rich in primary materials, of the sense of crisis that ran through Lutheran orthodoxy in the latter half of the century.

[4] R. J. Bast, *Honor Your Fathers. Catechisms and the Emergence of a Patriarchal Ideology in Germany 1400–1600* (Leiden, 1997). Traces the patriarchal discourse in catechetical literature from the fifteenth to the seventeenth centuries.

[5] P. Blickle (trans. Thomas Dunlap), *Communal Reformation. The Quest for Salvation in Sixteenth-Century Germany* (London, 1992). Translation of the influential German work cited in the original bibliography (no. 138). A full exposition of the Communal Reformation thesis, rooted in the details of the past.

[6] P. Blickle (trans. T. A. Brady, Jr), *Obedient Germans? A Rebuttal. A New View of German History* (Charlottesville, 1997). Important study of the strength of communal culture in Germany in the early modern period. Challenges accepted notions.

[7] P. Blickle, *Der Bauernkrieg. Die Revolution des gemeinen Mannes* (Munich, 1998). A short synthesis of many of the themes Blickle

has raised in related studies, including the relationship between the evangelical movement and the Revolution.

[8] P. Blickle (trans. B. Kümin), *From the Communal Reformation to the Revolution of the Common Man* (Leiden, 1998). Translated collection of articles, primarily dealing with the Communal Reformation and the Peasants' War.

[9] P. Blickle, 'Reformation and Communal Spirit: The Reply of the Theologians to Constitutional Change in the Late Middle Ages', in C. S. Dixon (ed.), *The German Reformation. The Essential Readings* (Oxford, 1999), 133–68. Translation of an article which effectively summarises the relationship between the reform movement and local political culture.

[10] T. A. Brady, Jr, *Protestant Politics. Jacob Sturm (1489–1553) and the German Reformation* (New Jersey, 1995). Magisterial account of how the Reformation affected political relations in the Empire. Approaches the theme from the perspective of Jacob Sturm and his imperial city of Strasbourg.

[11] T. A. Brady, Jr, *Communities, Politics and Reformation in Early Modern Europe* (Leiden, 1998). Collection which brings together many important articles on the social and political history of the Reformation.

[12] M. Brecht (trans. J. L. Schaaf), *Martin Luther. His Road to Reformation 1483–1521* (Minneapolis, 1985). First part of an extremely rich and authoritative three-volume biography of Luther's life. Not only important for its contribution to our understanding of Luther, but the entire Reformation movement.

[13] M. Brecht (trans. J. L. Schaaf), *Martin Luther. Shaping and Defining the Reformation 1521–1532* (Minneapolis, 1990).

[14] M. Brecht (trans. J. L. Schaaf), *Martin Luther. The Preservation of the Church 1532–1546* (Minneapolis, 1993).

[15] T. Brockmann, *Die Konzilsfrage in den Flug- und Streitschriften des deutschen Sprachraumes 1518–1563* (Göttingen, 1998). Careful examination of the published dialogue over the question of a church council. Reveals much of the broader theological issues.

[16] J. Burkhardt, *Das Reformationsjahrhundert. Deutsche Geschichte zwischen Medienrevolution und Institutionenbildung 1517–1617* (Stuttgart, 2002). Emphasises the historical importance of the Reformation as a media event as well as its contribution to the structural and institutional changes of the age.

[17] A. Nelson Burnett, *The Yoke of Christ. Martin Bucer and Christian Discipline* (Kirksville, 1994). Examines the ideas of church

discipline developed by the reformer Martin Bucer and his relations with the secular authorities.

[18] R. A. Cahill, *Philipp of Hesse and the Reformation* (Mainz, 2001). Valuable narrative history of the princely Reformation in the principality of Hesse.

[19] E. Cameron, *The European Reformation* (Oxford, 1991). The pre-eminent modern study of the European Reformation. Strong emphasis on theology, but in all aspects a very wide-ranging and authoritative synthesis.

[20] O. Chadwick, *The Early Reformation on the Continent* (Oxford, 2001). Recent collection of short chapters on important features of the early movement.

[21] M. U. Chrisman, *Conflicting Visions of Reform. German Lay Propaganda Pamphlets 1519–1530* (New Jersey, 1996). Lively survey of the evangelical pamphlet literature written by laymen. Divides the analysis into social categories.

[22] C. C. Christensen, *Princes and Propaganda. Electoral Saxon Art of the Reformation* (Kirksville, 1992). The use of art in the fabrication of confessional identity.

[23] A. G. Dickens and J. M. Tonkin, *The Reformation in Historical Thought* (London, 1985). Comprehensive survey of the historiography of the Reformation, from the earliest interpretations to the modern day.

[24] G. Dipple, *Antifraternalism and Anticlericalism in the German Reformation. Johann Eberlin von Günzburg and the Campaign against the Friars* (Aldershot, 1996). Study of the pamphlet literature of Eberlin von Günzburg, one of the most engaged and prolific of the early evangelical pamphleteers.

[25] C. S. Dixon, 'Political Culture and the Reformation in the Holy Roman Empire', *German History*, 14 (1996), 354–79. Review essay of recent works dealing with the political history of the Reformation.

[26] C. S. Dixon, 'The German Reformation and the Territorial Town: Reform Initiatives in Schwabach, 1523–1527', *German History*, 14 (1996), 123–40. Draws contrasts between the course of events in a territorial town and comparative events in the imperial cities.

[27] C. S. Dixon, *The Reformation and Rural Society. The Parishes of Brandenburg-Ansbach-Kulmbach 1528–1603* (Cambridge, 1996). Archive-based study of the Reformation in the rural parishes of a German principality. Examines the dynamic between the

intentions of the Lutheran state and the historical reality at the level of the parish.

[28] C. S. Dixon, 'Popular Astrology and Lutheran Propaganda in Reformation Germany', *History*, 84 (1999), 403–18. Analysis of popular astrological literature and how it served as a medium for the message of Lutheran orthodoxy.

[29] C. S. Dixon, 'The Princely Reformation in Germany', in A. Pettegree (ed.), *The Reformation World* (London, 2000), 146–68. Narrative study of the course of the Reformation movement in the German principalities.

[30] C. S. Dixon, *The Reformation in Germany* (Oxford, 2002). Survey volume on the history of the Reformation in the German lands. The most recent English overview of historiographical developments.

[31] R. van Dülmen, 'The Reformation and the Modern Age', in C. S. Dixon (ed.), *The German Reformation. The Essential Readings* (Oxford, 1999), 193–220. Translation of an important article that discusses the ways in which the Reformation contributed to the rise of modern society.

[32] M. U. Edwards, *Printing, Propaganda and Martin Luther* (London, 1994). Series of chapters dealing with the role of the press in the early movement. Speaks of the Reformation as a 'media event'.

[33] D. A. Eltis, 'Tensions between Clergy and Laity in Some Western German Cities in the Later Middle Ages', *Journal of Ecclesiastical History*, 43 (1992), 231–48. Illustrates the tradition of urban anticlericalism in place before the Luther affair.

[34] J. M. Estes, ' "Officium principis christiani." Erasmus and the Origins of the Protestant State Church', *Archiv für Reformationsgeschichte*, 83 (1992), 49–72. Locates many of the essential theoretical characteristics of the territorial church in the writings of Erasmus.

[35] R. von Friedeburg, *Self-Defence and Religious Strife in Early Modern Europe. England and Germany 1530–1680* (Aldershot, 2002). Valuable comparative investigation of the rise of Protestant resistance theories in their historical contexts.

[36] A. Friesen, *Thomas Muentzer, a Destroyer of the Godless. The Making of a Sixteenth-Century Religious Revolutionary* (Berkelely, 1990). Effective mix of biography and history, following the life of Müntzer while keeping broader events in view.

[37] P. Friess, *Die Außenpolitik der Reichsstadt Memmingen in der Reformationszeit (1517–1555)* (Memmingen, 1993). Study of the Reformation in the imperial city of Memmingen and how the

change of religion affected both domestic and imperial political relations.

[38] R. Fuhrmann, *Kirche und Dorf. Religiöse Bedürfnisse und kirchliche Stiftung auf dem Lande vor der Reformation* (Stuttgart, 1995). Careful study reveals that the rural communes assumed a significant role in religious affairs in the medieval period.

[39] H-J. Goertz, *Pfaffenhaß und groß Geschrei. Die reformatorischen Bewegungen in Deutschland 1517–1529* (Munich, 1987). Account of the early Reformation as a varied social movement, with particular stress on the role of anticlericalism.

[40] H-J. Goertz, 'Eine "bewegte" Epoche. Zur Heterogenität reformatorischer Bewegungen', in H. A. Oberman *et al.* (eds), *Reformiertes Erbe* (Zurich, 1993), 103–25. Argues in favour of a reform movement characterised by heterogeneity rather than Lutheran uniformity.

[41] H-J. Goertz, *Antiklerikalismus und Reformation. Sozialgeschichtliche Untersuchungen* (Göttingen, 1995). Close study of the different types of anticlericalism voiced in the early years.

[42] H-J. Goertz (trans. T. Johnson), *The Anabaptists* (London, 1996). Translation of an important German-language survey of the Anabaptist movement.

[43] J. Goodale, 'Pastors, Privation, and the Process of Reformation in Saxony', *Sixteenth Century Journal,* 33 (2002), 71–92. Source-based study of the conditions facing Lutheran pastors as they assumed office in rural parishes. Reveals the dynamics of social relations at the local level

[44] B. Gordon, 'The Changing Face of Protestant History and Identity in the Sixteenth Century', in B. Gordon (ed.), *Protestant History and Identity in Sixteenth-Century Europe* (Aldershot, 1996), 1–22. Introduction to an excellent collection of articles on the theme. Examines how Protestant thinkers fashioned a sense of history and identity.

[45] L. Grane, *Martinus noster. Luther in the German Reform Movement 1518–1521* (Mainz, 1994). Meticulous study of the initial reaction of the learned world to the Luther affair.

[46] K. von Greyerz, *Religion und Kultur. Europa 1500–1800* (Göttingen, 2000). Wide-ranging recent survey of religion and culture in Europe, integrating many modern historiographical insights.

[47] B. Hamm, 'The Urban Reformation in the Holy Roman Empire,' in T. A. Brady, H. Oberman and J. D. Tracy (eds), *Handbook of European History, 1400–1600: Late Middle Ages,*

Renaissance and Reformation (Leiden, 1995), Vol. 2, 193–220. Comprehensive summary of the themes associated with the urban Reformation, drawing on an extensive range of literature.

[48] B. Hamm, *Bürgertum und Glaube. Konturen der städtischen Reformation* (Göttingen, 1996). Sophisticated treatment of the Reformation in the imperial city of Nuremberg. Balances social forces with religious ideas, collectives with individuals, innovation with tradition.

[49] B. Hamm, 'Normative Centering in the Fifteenth and Sixteenth Centuries: Observations on Religiosity, Theology, and Iconology', *Journal of Early Modern History*, 3, 4, (1999), 307–54. Argues that late medieval religious culture was characterised in part by a desire to reduce the variety and complexity and capture the essence (the centre) of the faith.

[50] B. Hamm, 'What was the Reformation Doctrine of Justification?' in C. S. Dixon (ed.), *The German Reformation. The Essential Readings* (Oxford, 1999), 53–90. Identifies the principles of the evangelical doctrine of justification common to all Protestant traditions. Sophisticated fusion of theological and historical perspectives.

[51] B. Hamm, B. Moeller and D. Wendebourg, *Reformationstheorien. Ein kirchenhistorischer Disput über Einheit und Vielfalt der Reformation* (Göttingen, 1995). Debate between three leading church historians over the unity and the variety of the Reformation.

[52] H. Robinson Hammerstein (ed.), *The Transmission of Ideas in the Lutheran Reformation* (Dublin, 1989). Valuable collection of essays investigating the different methods and media used to disseminate the evangelical message.

[53] J. F. Harrington, *Reordering Marriage and Society in Reformation Germany* (Cambridge, 1995). Examines the impact of the Reformation on the laws and customs governing marriage.

[54] J. M. Headley, 'The Reformation as a Crisis in the Understanding of Tradition', *Archiv für Reformationsgeschichte*, 78 (1987), 5–22. Examines how Luther challenged inherited Catholic notions of tradition by placing such emphasis on the authority of the Word.

[55] T. Hohenberger, *Lutherische Rechtfertigungslehre in den reformatorischen Flugschriften der Jahre 1521–1522* (Tübingen, 1996). Traces the spread of evangelical ideas of justification in the early pamphlet literature. Supports the idea of Lutheran uniformity.

[56] S. Holtz, *Theologie und Alltag. Lehre und Leben in den Predigten der Tübinger Theologen 1550–1750* (Tubingen, 1993). Sheds light on the relationship between theology and social norms.

[57] R. Po-Chia Hsia (ed.), *The German People and the Reformation* (Ithaca, 1988). Collection of essays by leading scholars on the role of the parishioners in the movement.

[58] R. Po-Chia Hsia, *Social Discipline in the Reformation. Central Europe 1550–1750* (London, 1989). First English synthesis of work on social disciplining and confessionalisation. Effective balance of historical detail and general analysis.

[59] R. Po-Chia Hsia and R. W. Scribner (eds), *Problems in the Historical Anthropology of Early Modern Europe* (Wiesbaden, 1997). Contributions touching on the cultural aspects of Reformation history.

[60] S. C. Karant-Nunn, *Zwickau in Transition 1500–1547. The Reformation as an Agent of Change* (Columbus, 1987). Detailed and insightful look at how the change in religion could affect social, political, economic, and cultural relations in a relatively small city.

[61] S. C. Karant-Nunn, 'What was preached in the German Cities in the Early Years of the Reformation? *Wildwuchs* versus Lutheran Unity', in P. N. Bebb and S. Marshall (eds), *The Process of Change in Early Modern Europe* (Athens, Ohio, 1988). Argues that the early Reformation was characterised by a plurality of voices rather than Lutheran uniformity.

[62] S. C. Karant-Nunn, *The Reformation of Ritual. An Interpretation of Early Modern Germany* (London, 1997). Examines the impact of the Reformation on religious ritual during the century of Reformation. Suggests that many ritual traditions continued, though there was a transformation of meaning.

[63] T. Kaufmann, *Universität und lutherische Konfessionalisierung. Die Rostocker Theologieprofessoren und ihr Beitrag zur theologischen Bildung und kirchlichen Gestaltung im Herzogtum Mecklenburg zwischen 1500 und 1675* (Gütersloh, 1997). Detailed study of the Rostock theology faculty during the age of orthodoxy.

[64] R. Keen, 'Defending the Pious: Melanchthon and the Reformation in Albertine Saxony', *Church History*, 60 (1991), 180–95. Analysis of Melanchthon's ideas on the role of the Protestant princes in the evolution and maintenance of the territorial church.

[65] R. Keen, *Divine and Human Authority in Reformation Thought. German Theologians on Political Order 1520–1555* (Nieuwkoop, 1997). Comparative overview of the theological and political controversies on the relationship between secular and spiritual authority within the three main traditions (Catholic, Protestant and Anabaptist).

[66] J. Kittelson, *Toward an Established Church. Strasbourg from 1500 to the Dawn of the Seventeenth Century* (Mainz, 2000). Follows the long-term development of the Lutheran church in Strasbourg.

[67] W. Klassen, *Living at the End of the Ages. Apocalyptic Expectation in the Radical Reformation* (London, 1992). Surveys apocalypticism in Anabaptism by way of Thomas Müntzer, Hans Hergot, Augustine Bader and Jan Matthijs.

[68] R. Kolb, *For all the Saints. Changing Perceptions of Martyrdom and Sainthood in the Lutheran Reformation* (Macon, 1987). Examines how the Catholic legends associated with martyrdom were reworked by later generations of reformers to reflect Protestant Church history.

[69] R. Kolb, *Confessing The Faith. Reformers define the Church 1530–1580* (St Louis, 1991). Study of the making of the Lutheran confessions of the faith from the Confession of Augsburg to the Book of Concord.

[70] R. Kolb, *Martin Luther as Prophet, Teacher, Hero. Images of the Reformer 1520–1620* (Grand Rapids, 1999). Textual and iconographical analysis of the ways in which depictions of Luther changed over time.

[71] C. M. Koslofsky, *The Reformation of the Dead. Death and Ritual in Early Modern Germany 1450–1700* (Basingstoke, 2000). Examines how evangelical theology changed the ritual culture associated with burial.

[72] V. Leppin, 'Wie reformatorisch war die Reformation?' in *Zeitschrift für Theologie und Kirche*, 99 (2002), 162–76. Argues that the theological thought of the early Reformation cannot be harmonised under the principle of justification through faith.

[73] A. Levi, *Renaissance and Reformation. The Intellectual Genesis* (London, 2002). Magisterial treatment of the world of ideas in the age of Renaissance and Reformation. Speaks of resemblances and continuities rather than sudden shifts in thought.

[74] C. Lindberg, *The European Reformations* (Oxford, 1996). Extremely effective and readable narrative survey of the European Reformation movements.

[75] C. Lindberg (ed.), *The Reformation Theologians* (Oxford, 2002). Valuable collection of articles by leading scholars on the central Reformation theologians. Offers authoritative introductions to the religious ideas and the surrounding culture of the age.

[76] R. Marius, *Martin Luther. The Christian between God and Death* (Cambridge, 1999). Most recent English-language biography of Luther, with the emphasis on faith and death.

[77] P. Matheson, *The Rhetoric of the Reformation* (Edinburgh, 1998). Valuable analysis of how the evangelical authors used both the printing press and their language skills to create new genres and publicise their message.

[78] P. Matheson, *The Imaginative World of the Reformation* (Edinburgh, 2000). Thoughtful observations on how the change in religion brought about a change in perspectives.

[79] R. E. McLaughlin, *Caspar Schwenckfeld, a Reluctant Radical. His Life to 1540* (New Haven, 1986). Examines Schwenkfeld's theology in the context of historical and personal developments.

[80] C. Methuen, 'Securing the Reformation through Education: The Duke's Scholarship System of Sixteenth-Century Württemberg', *Sixteenth Century Journal,* 25 (1994), 841–51. Contribution of the Reformation to educational advances in Württemberg.

[81] B. Moeller, 'Das Berühmtwerden Luthers', *Zeitschrift für historische Forschung,* 15 (1988), 65–92. Pioneering study of the rise of Luther's celebrity and the fabrication of his image.

[82] B. Moeller, 'Die Rezeption Luthers in der frühen Reformation', *Luther Jahrbuch,* 57 (1990), 57–71. Public reactions to and perceptions of Luther in the early years.

[83] B. Moeller, 'What was Preached in German Towns in the Early Reformation?', in C. S. Dixon (ed.), *The German Reformation. The Essential Readings* (Oxford, 1999), 33–52. Translation of an important investigation into the theological content of the early evangelical sermons. Argues for a Lutheran uniformity.

[84] B. Moeller and K. Stackmann, *Städtische Predigt in der Frühzeit der Reformation. Eine Untersuchung deutscher Flugschriften der Jahre 1522 bis 1529* (Göttingen, 1996). Monography study of the theme discussed above, rich in pamphlet sources.

[85] K. Moxey, *Peasants, Warriors, and Wives. Popular Imagery in the Reformation* (Chicago, 1989). Study of the use of iconography during the early evangelical movement.

[86] W. D. Myers, *'Poor, Sinning Folk'. Confession and the Making of Consciences in Counter-Reformation Germany* (Ithaca, 1996). Styish and insightful examination of the culture of sacramental confession in the Catholic lands of southern Germany.

[87] B. Nischan, *Prince, People and Confession. The Second Reformation in Brandenburg* (Philadelphia, 1994). Meticulous survey of the nature of religious relations in Lutheran Brandenburg after the introduction of Calvinism.

[88] B. Nischan, 'Ritual and Protestant Identity in Late Reformation Germany', in B. Gordon (ed.), *Protestant History and Identity in*

111

Sixteenth-Century Europe (Aldershot, 1996), Vol. 2, 142–58. Illustrates how religious distinctions within the Protestant tradition were articulated and experienced through ritual.

[89] B. Nischan, 'Demarcating Boundaries: Lutheran Pericopic Sermons in the Age of Confessionalization', *Archiv für Reformationsgeschichte* 88 (1997), 199–216. Similar to the above, though with the focus on words rather than actions.

[90] B. Nischan, 'Germany after 1550', in A. Pettegree (ed.), *The Reformation World* (London, 2000), 386–407. Overview of the nature of confessional relations in Germany as Lutheranism and Calvinism struggled for dominance.

[91] H. Oelke, *Die Konfessionsbildung des 16. Jahrhunderts im Spiegel illustrierter Flugblätter* (Berlin, 1992). Examines a corpus of wood-cuts (141 in total) and how they functioned in the process of Protestant confessionalisation.

[92] W. O. Packull, 'In Search of the "Common Man" in Early German Baptist Ideology', *Sixteenth Century Journal*, 17 (1986), 51–67. Investigates the relationship between the Peasants' War and the Anabaptist movement.

[93] W. O. Packull, *Hutterite Beginnings. Communitarian Experiments during the Reformation* (Baltimore, 1995). Masterly overview of the history of the Anabaptist communities, with particular emphasis on the social dimensions of the movement.

[94] G. Parker, 'Success and Failure during the First Century of Reformation', *Past and Present*, 139 (1992), 43–82. Takes up and summarises the 'success and failure' debate, approaching the theme from an international perspective.

[95] A. Pettegree, *Europe in the Sixteenth Century* (Oxford, 2001). Very readable and perceptive narrative survey, drawing on recent literature.

[96] H. Rabe, *Reich und Glaubensspaltung. Deutschland 1500–1600* (Munich, 1989). Extremely comprehensive treatment of Germany during the century of Reformation. A wealth of information and insight.

[97] W. Reinhard, 'Reformation, Counter-Reformation, and the Early Modern State: A Reassessment', *Catholic Historical Review*, 75 (1989), 383–404. Examination of the relationship between the process of confessionalisation and the rise of the territorial powers.

[98] W. Reinhard, 'Pressures towards Confessionalization? Prolegomena to a Theory of the Confessional Age', in C. S. Dixon (ed.), *The German Reformation. The Essential Readings* (Oxford,

1999), 169–92. Translation of a very influential article on the theme of confessionalisation. Argues that religious developments had a direct and lasting impact on the social and political world.

[99] T. Robisheaux, *Rural Society and the Search for Order in Early Modern Germany* (Cambridge, 1989). Important investigation of political relations in the territory of Hohenlohe during the age of Reformation.

[100] L. Roper, *The Holy Household. Women and Morals in Reformation Augsburg* (Oxford, 1989). Innovative study of how the Reformation affected gender relations. Suggests that in many spheres, the household in particular, the patriarchal model was confirmed.

[101] L. Roper, 'Sexual Utopianism in the German Reformation', *Journal of Ecclesiastical History*, 42 (1991), 394–418. Examines the relationship between sexuality and holiness, examining a range of views, from the mainstream reformers to the Anabaptists.

[102] L. Roper, *Oedipus and the Devil. Witchcraft, Sexuality and Religion in Early Modern Europe* (London, 1995). Collection of essays on the perception and understanding of sexuality in the early modern period.

[103] M. Rubin, *Corpus Christi. The Eucharist in Late-Medieval Culture* (Cambridge, 1991). Thoughtful and imaginative study of popular and learned attitudes to the Eucharist on the eve of the Reformation.

[104] H-C. Rublack, 'New Patterns of Christian Life', in T. A. Brady, Jr, H. A. Oberman, and J. D. Tracy (eds), *Handbook of European History 1400–1600: Late Middle Ages, Renaissance and Reformation* (Leiden, 1995), Vol. 2, 585–605. A skillful synthesis of the themes and the literature relating to the social and cultural impact of the Reformation on German life.

[105] E. Rummel, *The Humanist-Scholastic Debate in the Renaissance and Reformation* (London, 1995). Learned and entertaining study of the points of agreement and debate between humanists and scholastics during the Reformation era.

[106] E. Rummel, *The Confessionalization of Humanism in Reformation Germany* (Oxford, 2000). Similar to the above, though with a more detailed discussion of how the religious issues divided the intellectual communities.

[107] H. Schilling (trans. S. Burnett), *Religion, Political Culture, and the Emergence of Early Modern Society: Essays in German and Dutch*

113

History (Leiden, 1992). Translation of an important and influential series of articles. Includes discussion of confessionalisation, Second Reformation, and urban reform.

[108] H. Schilling, *Die Stadt in der frühen Neuzeit* (Munich, 1993). Synthesis of the themes and literature relating to urban history in the early modern period.

[109] H. Schilling, 'Confessional Europe', in T. A. Brady, H. Oberman, and J. D. Tracy (eds), *Handbook of European History 1400–1600. Late Middle Ages, Renaissance and Reformation* (Leiden, 1995), Vol. 2, 641–81. Overview of the confessionalisation debate, both a concise presentation of the thesis and a summary of related literature.

[110] A. Schindling and W. Ziegler (eds), *Die Territorien des Reichs im Zeitalter der Reformation und Konfessionalisierung 1500–1650* (7 Vols, Münster, 1989–98). Extremely valuable multi-volume collection of articles on the reform movements in the German territories during the confessional age. The first point of reference for an introduction to the many territorial histories and the related literature.

[111] H. R. Schmidt, *Reichsstädte, Reich und Reformation. Korporative Religionspolitik 1521–1529/30* (Stuttgart, 1986). Important study of urban politics during the early stage of the Reformation movement, with particular emphasis on events in Nuremberg. Examines both domestic and imperial developments.

[112] H. R. Schmidt, *Dorf und Religion. Reformierte Sittenzucht in Berner Landgemeinden der Frühen Neuzeit* (Stuttgart, 1995). Investigation of the state of morality and moral norms in the rural parishes belonging to Bern. Challenges the assumption that the state imposed a lasting moral order.

[113] L. Schorn-Schütte, *Die Reformation: Vorgeschichte – Verlauf – Wirkung* (Munich, 1996). Succinct survey of the Reformation movement and its associated historiography.

[114] L. Schorn-Schütte, *Evangelische Geistlichkeit in der Frühneuzeit. Deren Anteil an der Entfaltung frühmoderner Staatlichkeit und Gesellschaft* (Gütersloh, 1996). Meticulous and important study of the rise of the Protestant clergy. Ranges widely to address essential questions relating to social relations and political developments.

[115] L. Schorn-Schütte, 'Priest, Preacher, Pastor: Research on Clerical Office in Early Modern Europe', *Central European History*, 33 (2000), 1–39. Summary of recent work on the early modern clergy in Europe, with an overview of research themes.

[116] W. Schulze, 'Vom Gemeinnutz zum Eigennutz. Über den Normenwandel in der ständischen Geschichte der frühen Neuzeit', *Historische Zeitschrift*, 243 (1986), 591–622. Important article which touches on the relationship between confessional developments and social norms.

[117] T. Scott, *Thomas Müntzer. Theology and Revolution in the German Reformation* (Basingstoke, 1989). Biography of the radical reformer that handles all aspects of his life with authority, from theology to social and political developments.

[118] T. Scott, *Society and Economy in Germany 1300–1600* (Basingstoke, 2002). The best modern survey of the theme, drawing on the most recent literature.

[119] T. Scott and B. Scribner (eds), *The German Peasants' War: A History in Documents* (New Jersey, 1991). A very informative and lively selection of documents translated and edited by the two leading authorities in the English world.

[120] R. W. Scribner, *Popular Culture and Popular Movements in Reformation Germany* (London, 1987). Collection of articles on a variety of themes. Innovative and imaginative, and central to modern ideas about the cultural history of the Reformation. [Includes from original bibliography nos. 8, 33, 35a, 44, 46, 47, 66, 68, 69.]

[121] B. Scribner, 'The Impact of the Reformation on Daily Life', in Gerhard Jaritz (ed.), *Mensch und Objekt im Mittelalter und in der frühen Neuzeit: Leben-Alltag-Kultur* (Vienna, 1990). Examines how the process of reform affected religious culture at the parish level. Projects a complex dynamic, but stresses a general lack of impact on traditional affairs.

[122] B. Scribner, 'The Reformation Movements in Germany', in G. R. Elton (ed.), *The New Cambridge Modern History* (Cambridge, 1990), Vol. 2, 69–93. Overview of the evangelical movement and the gradual institutionalisation of reform.

[123] B. Scribner, 'The Reformation and the Religion of the Common People,' in H. R. Guggisberg and G. G. Krodel (eds), *Die Reformation in Deutschland und Europa. Interpretationen und Debatten* (Gütersloh, 1993), 221–41. Nuanced investigation of the impact of reform on parish life. Speaks more of continuity than change.

[124] B. Scribner, *Varieties of Reformation* (London, 1993). Compact survey of the different types of Reformation imagined in the early years.

115

[125] R. W. Scribner, *For the Sake of Simple Folk. Popular Propaganda for the German Reformation* (Oxford, 1994). Second edition of the original text, with an additional chapter and an updated bibliography.

[126] R. W. Scribner, 'Heterodoxy, Literacy and Print in the early German Reformation', in P. Biller (ed.), *Heresy and Literacy 1000–1530* (Cambridge, 1994), 155–78. Examines the role of the printed word and the relationship between literacy and the movement.

[127] B. Scribner, 'The Reformation, Popular Magic, and the "Disenchantment" of the World', in C. S. Dixon (ed.), *The German Reformation. The Essential Readings* (Oxford, 1999), 259–80. Argues against the notion that the Reformation represented a process of descralisation and thus contributed to the rise of a more rational, secular modern world.

[128] R. W. Scribner (L. Roper, ed.), *Religion and Culture in Germany (1400–1800)* (Leiden, 2001). Recent collection of essays. Range widely, but the main themes include studies of popular belief, religious perception, social relations and reform, and the dynamics of local cultures and beliefs.

[129] C. A. Snyder, *Anabaptist History and Theology. An Introduction* (Kitchener, 1995). Thoughtful survey that does justice to the heterogeneity of the tradition.

[130] L. Spitz, *Luther and German Humanism* (Aldershot, 1996). Collection of essays that deals with the relationship between the Reformation (and Luther in particular) and the Humanist movement.

[131] L. Spitz, *The Reformation. Education and History* (Aldershot, 1997). Valuable collection of the role of Protestant reform on the history of education.

[132] J. Stayer, *The German Peasants' War and Anabaptist Community of Goods* (Montreal, 1991). Treatment of the relationship between the evangelical movement, the Peasants' War, and Anabaptism. Argues that there was a 'significant connection' between Anabaptism and the War.

[133] G. Strauss, *Law, Resistance and the State. The Opposition to Roman Law in Reformation Germany* (Princeton, 1986). Examines the reception of Roman law in Germany during the early modern period. Excellent survey, with many insights on the Reformation.

[134] G. Strauss, 'Ideas of *Reformatio* and *Renovatio* from the Middle Ages to the Reformation', in T. A. Brady, H. Oberman, and

J. D. Tracy (eds), *Handbook of European History, 1400–1600: Late Middle Ages, Renaissance and Reformation* (Leiden, 1995), Volume II, 1–30. Discussion of the various meanings of the term 'reformation' on the eve of the Luther affair.

[135] R. N. Swanson, *Religion and Devotion in Europe c. 1215–c. 1515* (Cambridge, 1995). Most recent English overview of religious culture in the medieval age. Very skillful treatment of the different levels of experience and interaction.

[136] H. Talkenberger, *Sintflut. Prophetie und Zeitgeschehen in Texten und Holzschnitten astrologischer Flugschriften 1488–1528* (Tübingen, 1990). Examines the run of pamphlets and woodcuts dealing with the predicted flood of 1524.

[137] B. Tolley, *Pastors and Parishioners in Württemberg during the Late Reformation 1581–1621* (Stanford, 1995). Archive-based survey of the state of religion in some rural parishes of Württemberg. Suggests the impact of the Reformation was ambiguous.

[138] J. D. Tracy, *European Reformations 1450–1650* (Oxford, 1999). Illustrates the continuities between the Reformation and the medieval age, and situates reform in the social and political context.

[139] R. L. Vice, 'Iconoclasm in Rothenburg ob der Tauber in 1525', *Archiv für Reformationsgeschichte*, 89 (1998), 55–78. Study of the relationship between the reform movement, iconoclasm, and the Peasants' War in the territory of an imperial city.

[140] G. Vogler, 'Reformation als Alternative – Alternativen der Reformation', in G. Vogler (ed.), *Wegscheiden der Reformation. Alternatives Denken vom 16. bis zum 18. Jahrhundert* (Weimar, 1994), 11–21. Müntzer's notion of Reformation in contrast to Luther's. Bears out the idea of variety rather than uniformity.

[141] L. Palmer Wandel, *Voracious Idols and Violent Hands. Iconoclasm in Reformation Zurich, Strasbourg, and Basel* (Cambridge, 1995). Investigation of iconoclasm in the local setting, reading the sources against the social and political context.

[142] S. Westphal, *Frau und lutherische Konfessionalisierung. Eine Untersuchung zum Fürstentum Pfalz-Neuburg 1542–1614* (Frankfurt, 1994). The effect of the Reformation on the standing of women in the principality of Neuburg. A mixed legacy, though no fundamental change for the better.

[143] P. H. Wilson, *The Holy Roman Empire 1495–1806* (London, 1999). Excellent short survey of the political constitution of the Empire, with a wide range of modern literature in support.

[144] J. C. Wolfart, *Religion, Government and Political Culture in Early Modern Germany: Lindau 1520–1628* (Basingstoke, 2002). Innovative study of the relationship between the Reformation and political culture in the imperial city of Lindau.

[145] E. Wolgast, 'Formen landesfürstlicher Reformationen in Deutschland. Kursachsen – Württemberg/Brandenburg-Kurpfalz', in L. Grane and K. Hørby (eds), *Die dänische Reformation vor ihrem internationalen Hintergrund* (Göttingen, 1990), 57–90. Speaks of the models of territorial Reformation and their common features.

[146] E. Wolgast, 'Die deutschen Territorialfürsten und die frühe Reformation', in S. E. Buckwalter and B. Moeller (eds), *Die frühe Reformation in Deutschland als Umbruch* (Gütersloh, 1998), 407–34. Suggests that the princes were rather slow to respond, though essential for the survival of the movement.

[147] W. J. Wright, *Capitalism, the State and the Lutheran Reformation. Sixteenth-Century Hesse* (Columbus, 1988). Examination of the Hessian social and economic policies and the relationship to religious reform.

[148] H. Wunder, *Die bäuerliche Gemeinde in Deutschland* (Göttingen, 1986). Excellent synthesis of recent work on the rural communes in Germany.

[149] K. Eldyss Sorensen Zapalac, *'In his Image and Likeness'. Political Iconography and Religious Change in Regensburg 1500–1600* (Ithaca, 1990). Nuanced look at how the Reformation affected the iconography of an imperial city, from notions of justice and politics to gender relations.

[150] C. Zika, 'Hosts, Processions and Pilgrimages in Fifteenth-Century Germany', *Past and Present*, 118 (1988), 25–64. Examines the many meanings and functions of the Host in late-medieval Germany and what it reveals of clerical power.

Index